A Rainbow Book

Protecting Your Family's Assets

*How to Legally Use Medicaid
to Pay for Nursing Home
and Assisted Living Care*

–SECOND EDITION–

John R. Frazier J.D., LL.M.

Rainbow Books, Inc.
FLORIDA

Protecting Your Family's Assets in Florida:
How to Legally Use Medicaid to Pay for Nursing Home and Assisted Living Care
SECOND EDITION © 2012 by John R. Frazier J.D., LL.M.

Softcover ISBN 978-1-56825-129-5
ePub (ebook) ISBN 978-1-56825130-1

Published by

Rainbow Books, Inc.
P. O. Box 430
Highland City, FL 33846-0430

Editorial Offices and Wholesale/Distributor Orders

Telephone: (863) 648-4420
Email: RBIbooks@aol.com
www.RainbowBooksInc.com

Author's Website

www.EstateLegalPlanning.com

Individuals' Orders

Toll-free Telephone (800) 431-1579
www.Amazon.com
www.AllBookStores.com
www.BookCH.com

The paper used in this publication meets the minimum requirements of the American National Standard for Information Sciences—Permanence of Paper for Printed Library Materials, ANSI Z39.48-1984.

Second Edition 2012
16 15 14 13 12   7 6 5 4 3 2 1

Printed in the United States of America.

To my parents, J. Richard Frazier and Anne R. Frazier,
and my grandparents, Richard O. Frazier and Marian R. Frazier,
whose life-long dedication to higher education
served as an inspiration for this book.

CONTENTS

Acknowledgments

A special appreciation is due my mentor and friend Joseph F. Pippen, Jr. for his wisdom and guidance throughout my legal career. I would also like to thank my friends Henry Harlow and Jamie Primeau for their efforts in making this book a reality. Lastly, to my publisher Betty Wright and her key team member at Rainbow Books, Betsy Lampe, whose editing and design efforts have been critical to the success of my books.

An Overview
of the Benefits of Medicaid

The average private-pay, room-and-board rate at a skilled nursing facility in Florida costs between $5,000 and $7,000 per month. Some facilities charge even more. There are additional charges for items and services, such as laundry, transportation to and from the facility, incidentals, and over-the-counter/prescription medications. It is not uncommon for total private-pay costs at nursing facilities to exceed $6,000 per month. Many families cannot afford to pay such excessive amounts – which can exceed $70,000 per year – for private-pay residents at skilled nursing facilities.

The Florida Medicaid program can offer a solution to the high cost of nursing home and assisted living care; however, an individual must qualify for Medicaid assistance. The problem with qualifying for assistance from Medicaid is that the Medicaid programs have strict asset and income limitations. With proper planning, however, even individuals whose assets and income greatly exceed the limits for Medicaid can qualify for benefits.

When a nursing home resident qualifies for Medicaid, the program will pay for the cost of room and board at the nursing home. Medicaid requires that the resident's gross monthly income (before deductions for witholdings, such as taxes and insurance) be paid to the facility (for an unmarried nursing home resident). The nursing home resident is allowed to keep $35 per month from his/her income. There is also a reduction for any monthly health insurance expense.

The Medicaid rate amount paid by the nursing home resident is referred to as the *patient responsibility*. The patient responsibility may be even lower if the Medicaid applicant is married. For an unmarried person, patient responsibility equals the following:

Resident's Gross Monthly Income

subtract $35/Month (personal cash)

subtract Cost of Resident's Health Insurance (if any)

equals Amount of Resident's Income to be Paid to the Nursing Home (patient responsibility)

The Medicaid program is also a comprehensive health insurance program. It pays for the cost of a nursing home or assisted living resident's inpatient and outpatient medical care, hospitalization, surgery, dialysis, transportation to and from hospitals and physician's offices, psychiatric care and counseling, medical supplies, and over-the-counter/prescription medications. Under certain circumstances, the Florida Medicaid program may also cover the cost of dental care, hearing aids and eyeglasses.

Because the requirements for Medicaid are so complex, some sort of advice will be necessary to move through the maze of agencies and their strictures. One choice is certainly an elder attorney, who will have up-to-date information from the various agencies involved.

This book includes many facts, figures, examples, and references to help the Medicaid seekers in their quest. After reading it, you may decide to read further or seek professional help. The latter is always available, but should be an attorney who practices in elder law, or a life care attorney who is competent in all aspects of this thorny problem. Financial planners and even social workers can steer an elder or his family in the right direction, but to explore all the avenues for maintaining a family's wealth in the face of staggering medical costs, an elder attorney is the best choice.

Read on to see why this is true. It is not an accident that this book is titled, *Protecting Your Family's Assets in Florida: How to Legally Use Medicaid to Pay for Nursing Home and Assisted Living Care*. No individuals want to spend all their capital resources on nursing home care; however, many feel that they have no alternative. This book gives the reader alternative after alternative.

CHAPTER 1

The Three Florida Agencies that Handle Medicaid

While Medicaid is a federal program, the program is managed by state agencies, each of which sets its own rules for eligibility and services. With regard to nursing home and assisted living care in Florida, the following three state agencies are responsible for handling Medicaid:

- The Florida Department of Children and Families (DCF)
- The Agency for Health Care Administration (AHCA)
- The Florida Department of Elder Affairs (DOEA)

The Florida Department of Children and Families (DCF)

The Florida Department of Children and Families offers many helpful programs to Florida residents. These programs include community based care, child care, adoption, child abuse prevention, domestic violence, foster care, mental health, refugee, and substance abuse – to name only a few areas of assistance.

The Florida DCF *Adult Services Unit* evaluates the financial part of an individual's Medicaid application for either nursing home or assisted living care. In addition, the Adult Services Unit provides adult protective services, placement services for elderly individuals, home and community care for disabled individuals, and home and community services for adults.

The Agency for Health Care Administration (AHCA)

The Agency for Health Care Administration is another Florida government agency involved with Medicaid. AHCA licenses health care facilities, including hospitals, skilled nursing facilities, assisted living facilities, health care clinics, clinical laboratories, as well as many other facilities that provide medical care in Florida.

AHCA also takes part in the financial side of Medicaid, which includes paying a Medicaid recipient's health care providers. AHCA also recovers Medicaid benefits that have been improperly paid to health care providers, investigates suspected Medicaid fraud, and recovers other types of misplaced Medicaid benefits.

The Florida Department of Elder Affairs (DOEA)

The Florida Department of Elder Affairs is the Florida government agency that provides programs specifically to assist elderly Florida residents. Two of the more familiar DOEA programs are the Florida Association of Area Agencies on Aging (with 11 area agencies in Florida) and the Long-Term Care Ombudsman Program.

Another, lesser-known program, is the Comprehensive Assessment and Review for Long Term Care Services (CARES). This group processes the health care portion of an individual's Medicaid application. The CARES team determines whether a Medicaid applicant meets the basic medical criteria for Medicaid assistance, either in a nursing home or in an assisted living facility. (These medical criteria will be discussed in more detail in the next section of this book.)

CHAPTER 2

The Three Tests
for Medicaid Qualification

There are three basic requirements, or tests, for Medicaid in Florida. These tests are:

- The Medical Test
- The Asset Test
- The Income Test

Medicaid applicants must meet the requirements of all three tests, whether they are applying for the Institutional Care Program, the Medicaid Waiver Program, or the Long Term Care Diversion Program. (Details on these three programs are discussed in later chapters.)

The Medical Test

The medical test helps the State of Florida determine whether a nursing home resident, or an assisted living resident, qualifies *medically* for Medicaid assistance. You might assume that a person who resides in a nursing home or assisted living facility would automatically be qualified for Medicaid; however, this is not necessarily true.

If a person is healthy enough to live independently at home, then the person would generally *not* pass the medical test for Medicaid. Medicaid assistance is for the applicant who has an actual medical *need* to be in a nursing home or assisted living facility.

Whether or not a person has an actual medical need for Medicaid is determined by the Florida Department of Elder Affairs CARES unit. A CARES caseworker evaluates Medicaid applicants based on criteria referred to as the *Activities of Daily Living* (ADLs). ADLs are tasks you and I do every day — without assistance — such as:

- bathe
- eat
- dress and undress
- move around
- get into and out of bed
- use the toilet

If a person can perform all of these activities *without* assistance, it would be very unlikely that the person would meet ADL criteria for Medicaid. However, if a person were unable to perform any of the ADLs, without the assistance of another person, then the person would most likely meet the ADL criteria for Medicaid.

Example: Jessica is a 98-year-old woman who has lived in an assisted living facility for the past three years. She has been diagnosed with dementia, diabetes, coronary artery disease, high blood pressure, and a fractured hip. She is unable to walk, feed herself, dress, or toilet without assistance. Because of her difficulty walking and keeping her balance while she was a resident in the assisted living facility, she fell and fractured her hip.

Over the past year, she developed a history of falling. Her doctor now states that after Jessica leaves the hospital for treatment for her fractured hip, she will need to be placed in a rehabilitation center and later admitted to a skilled nursing facility for long-term care.

The rehabilitation center recommended by the doctor is also a long-term skilled nursing facility, and the facility accepts both Medicaid and Medicare funding.

Jessica will be evaluated by the CARES caseworker to establish whether or not she would pass the medical test for Medicaid. The CARES caseworker will most likely determine that Jessica meets "the medically necessary level of care" for all three Florida Medicaid programs.

Jessica's age, her various health problems – and because she is unable to perform the activities of daily living without assistance – help establish that Jessica is medically qualified for all three Florida Medicaid programs. In other words, Jessica truly *needs* a great deal of medical assistance to live.

The Asset Test

The second test, required for a Medicaid applicant to be accepted by Medicaid, is the asset test. Assets are the entire property of a person, including a home, cars, money – everything of real value that a person owns.

Under current law, a single Medicaid applicant is allowed no more than $2,000 in *countable* assets. If the applicant is married, the applicant's community spouse is allowed to have up to $113,640 in countable assets in 2012. If *both* spouses are applying for Medicaid, then both spouses are allowed to have no more than $3,000 in combined countable assets.

A countable asset is one that counts toward the asset limit, and a non-countable asset is one that does not count toward the asset limit. Under current law, the primary non-countable assets are the following:

One home in Florida (up to $525,000 in value). The home can be a traditional house, a condominium, or a mobile home. Homes in other states may also be exempt under certain conditions. If a person's home is located in another state with which Florida has an interstate agreement, the home in the other state will be exempt. The State of Florida currently has interstate agreements with the following states: Alabama, Arkansas, California, Georgia, Idaho, Iowa, Kansas, Kentucky, Louisiana, Maryland, Minnesota, Mississippi, New Jersey, New Mexico, North Dakota, Ohio, South Dakota, Tennessee, Texas, and West Virginia.[1] If the applicant's home is located outside of the State of Florida, and there is no interstate agreement with the state where the property is located, the home will be a countable asset.

Also related to whether the home is exempt is the Medicaid applicant's intent to return home. Generally, the caseworkers at the Florida Department of Children and Families take the view that the intent to return home is *presumed* to exist. If the Medicaid applicant has taken some type of affirmative step (such as signing a written statement) to indicate the intent to return home no longer exists, then the home will no longer continue to be an exempt asset.

Although the intent to return home is generally presumed by most DCF caseworkers, other scenarios may affect their evaluation. If the Medicaid applicant has never lived in the home prior to admission to the nursing facility or assisted living facility, the caseworker may have grounds for taking the position that the intent to return home does not exist. The caseworker can then classify the home as a countable asset. If such a situation were to occur, a lawyer might be able to argue, on appeal, that this action by the state could be considered as unlawful discrimination under the Florida Constitution or the United States Constitution.

In some cases, the Medicaid applicant or his spouse may own more than one piece of real estate. If a Medicaid applicant owns a home in Florida, but also owns several lots of land either in Florida or outside of Florida, those extra lots of land will be countable assets.

One way to deal with the problem of "extra" countable real estate is to list the property for sale with a written listing agreement. If the property is marketed for sale – with a good faith effort to sell – then the property will become a non-countable asset. This enables the Medicaid applicant to obtain Medicaid benefits immediately.[2]

Example: Judy is a Florida resident applying for Medicaid in a skilled nursing facility.

Judy owns a mobile home in Florida worth $50,000, and a lot of vacant land in Ohio worth $10,000. The mobile home in Florida is exempt because it is her home, and she intends to return home.

Assuming that all other tests are met, the $10,000 lot of land prevents Judy from qualifying for Medicaid, because the $10,000 lot of land is a countable asset. If Judy lists the Ohio lot for sale at fair market value, with a written listing agreement, the lot then becomes a non-countable asset. Judy can then immediately qualify for Medicaid benefits.

Another real estate complication occurs when the Medicaid applicant owns more than one residence. For example, assume that a Medicaid applicant owns a condominium unit which is his or her primary residence, and the Medicaid applicant also owns another condominium unit. The condominium being used as the primary residence would be a non-countable asset (up to $525,000 in value); however, the second condominium would be a countable asset.

As previously mentioned, one way to change the second condominium to a non-countable asset would be to list the property for sale with a written listing agreement. There is a second strategy available that will convert the second condominium into a non-countable asset: under Florida law, if property is *rented* for fair market value, then the real estate becomes a non-countable asset.[3]

Example: Stephanie is a 93-year-old widow who owns a home in Polk County, Florida, and a vacant condominium unit on Clearwater Beach.

Stephanie has recently been admitted to a skilled nursing facility because of a stroke that has paralyzed her right side. Her doctor has indicated that she needs long-term care.

The homestead property in Polk County is exempt, but the vacant condo in Clearwater Beach is a countable asset, which will prevent Stephanie from obtaining Medicaid benefits.

If the fair market rental value of the condominium is determined to be $1,800 per month, and Stephanie rents the condominium for $1,800 per month, the condominium then becomes a non-countable asset.

Assuming that Stephanie meets all other eligibility require-ments for Medicaid, Stephanie will obtain Medicaid benefits immediately.

Other assets that are usually non-countable include:

One car. Multiple cars can be exempt if the other cars are seven years old (or older) and are not luxury vehicles. Other exempt assets include:

Household items and furnishings.

Clothing and many personal effects.

An irrevocable funeral service contract or cremation contract. In addition to an irrevocable funeral or cremation contract, each spouse is allowed to have a bank account referred to as a "burial savings ac-count," up to a maximum of $2,500 for each spouse.

One burial plot for each spouse.

Life insurance with no cash value (such as group or term life insurance) is also a non-countable asset. Life insurance with cash value may also be a non-countable asset, if the face amount of all life insurance policies is $2,500 or less (or $2,500 or less for each spouse).

The Income Test

The third requirement to qualify for Medicaid benefits is the income test. The following items are considered income by the State of Florida:

- Social Security payments
- pensions
- interest
- dividends
- annuity payments
- rent

Some states have income restrictions for Medicaid qualification, and some states do not. States that have no income limit for Medicaid qualification are referred to as "Medically Needy" states. Florida is not a "Medically Needy" state.

Other states have an income limit. These states are referred to as "Income Cap" states. Florida is an "Income Cap" state. The income limit in income cap states is tied to the Federal Supplemental Security Income (SSI) monthly benefit for the year. Each year, the SSI benefit level is adjusted by the Social Security Administration. (In 2012, the SSI benefit level is $698 per month.)

In states that have a Medicaid income cap, the income cap limit is 300% of the SSI benefit level. This means that, in 2012, the Medicaid income cap for states with an income cap is $2,094 in gross (before taxes or other deductions) monthly income. This means that a Medicaid applicant who has monthly gross income that exceeds $2,094 per month — in an income cap state — fails the income test.

Federal law has, however, provided a way to help a Medicaid applicant (with gross income over $2,094 per month in 2012) to obtain Medicaid qualification. In 1993, Congress passed a law called the Omnibus Budget Reconciliation Act (OBRA '93). Among many other changes, OBRA '93 authorized certain trusts to be established by Medicaid applicants so they can obtain Medicaid benefits.[4] The type of trust that can be used is a "Qualified Income Trust" (also known as an "Income-Only Trust" — formerly known as a "Miller Trust"[5]).

Qualified Income Trust

There are several requirements, both federal and state, of a Qualified Income Trust. First, the trust must be irrevocable (except to appoint new trustees, or comply with changes in the law) which means the trust can't be changed. Also, the trust must name the State of Florida as the primary beneficiary of any funds left in the trust, at the time of the Medicaid recipient's death. Each Qualified Income Trust will be reviewed by DCF legal counsel, at the office where Medicaid benefits are applied for, to ensure that the income trust meets all mandatory legal criteria.

A Qualified Income Trust may be established by the Medicaid applicant, the spouse of the Medicaid applicant, or an attorney-in-fact with a properly drafted power of attorney. If there is no spouse, no attorney-in-fact, and if the Medicaid applicant is incapacitated, a court can authorize the establishment of an Income Trust in a guardianship proceeding.

An attorney-in-fact must have a durable power of attorney to establish a Qualified Income Trust for a Medicaid applicant. Durable power of attorney is discussed in Chapter 7. According to Florida statutes for a durable power of attorney document, the document must contain a specific authorization for the attorney-in-fact to establish a trust.[6]

Many power of attorney documents do not contain such a grant of authority to establish a trust. If the principal (the person giving the authority to the attorney-in-fact) has lost capacity and can no longer sign a new power of attorney document (and there is no spouse), someone would have to petition a court to establish the Qualified Income Trust.

In recent years, the legal offices of the Department of Children and Families have accepted a "general grant" of authority, stated in a power of attorney, to establish a Qualified Income Trust. (The criteria for powers of attorney changed on October 1, 2011. This issue will be discussed in more detail in chapter 7.) This should reflect a statewide policy change; however, exercise caution if the durable power of attorney contains only a "general grant" of authority and not a specific authorization to establish a trust.

After the Qualified Income Trust has been established, several other steps must be followed to insure Medicaid qualification. As a general rule, irrevocable trusts are required to have an Employer Identification Number (EIN), not the applicant's Social Security number. Some banks will require an EIN for a Qualified Income Trust. An employer identification number is applied for with the Internal Revenue Service using IRS Form SS-4, either in its paper form, online at www.irs.gov, or by calling the IRS at 1-800-829-4933.

After the EIN is established with the IRS, the next step is to establish a checking account for the Qualified Income Trust. The State of Florida requires the checking account be titled in the name of the trust. The state also requires the Qualified Income Trust checking account be "funded" every month with a certain amount of the Medicaid applicant's income. This means that a certain dollar amount of the Medicaid applicant's income must be deposited into the Qualified Income Trust checking account each month. The minimum monthly funding requirement equals the gross income minus (-) the income cap of $2,094.

Generally speaking, the Medicaid applicant's *gross* monthly income (minus the personal needs allowance and minus any health insurance premium) should be deposited into the Qualified Income Trust checking account. The gross monthly income is the Medicaid applicant's "net" monthly income, plus any withholding for items such as:

- federal income tax
- health insurance premiums
- life insurance deductions
- survivor benefit pay withholdings
- alimony
- Medicare Part B premiums

As a general rule, an unmarried Medicaid applicant will get a deduction from the patient responsibility for:

- secondary health insurance premiums
- a $35/per month deduction for the personal needs allowance (for the Institutional Care Program
- a $54/per month deduction for the personal needs allowance (for the Medicaid Waiver Program)

Though it may seem unfair, the State of Florida will not allow a deduction from the patient responsibility for items such as life insurance, survivor benefit pay, federal income taxes or alimony paid to former spouses.

For most individuals, there is a $99.90 Medicare Part B premium that the Federal Government withholds each month from most individuals' monthly Social Security benefit. After a person qualifies for Medicaid, this premium will no longer be withheld. However, it may take several months for the premium deduction to stop. The change will be retroactive to the first month that the Medicaid applicant qualifies for Medicaid benefits.

It is important to note, the State of Florida does not *absolutely* require that all of the Medicaid applicant's gross income be deposited into the Qualified Income Trust checking account. The calculation for the minimum monthly funding rule of the Qualified Income Trust is the gross monthly income minus the income gap equals the minimum monthly funding amount:

Gross Monthly Income

minus Income Cap

equals Minimum Monthly Funding Amount

The reason for depositing the gross monthly income is that if the Medicaid applicant under-funds the Qualified Income Trust in any given month — even by one cent — the Medicaid applicant will not be qualified for Medicaid in that month.

Another difficulty in following the minimum funding requirement rule is that it can often be very difficult to determine the exact monthly gross income amount. Other open bank accounts owned by the Medicaid applicant will often generate small amounts of interest income, which must be added to calculate the exact gross income amount. The safest thing for the Medicaid applicant to do, therefore, is to fund the Qualified Income Trust checking account each month with the gross income (minus the personal needs allowance and minus any health insurance premium).

A single Medicaid applicant who is a nursing home resident will be required to pay all of his or her gross income to the nursing facility (minus the $35 personal needs allowance and premiums for any secondary health insurance). Therefore, if any items are going to be withheld from funding the Income Trust each month, they should be limited to the $35 personal needs allowance for nursing home residents ($54 for Medicaid Waiver applicants) and any premiums paid for secondary health insurance.

Example: Jeannie Smith, a widow, is an 83-year-old resident of Seminole County, Florida.

She has recently fallen and broken her pelvis. The traumatic injury has also triggered the onset of dementia, and Jeannie can no longer live by herself. Her physician is recommending long-term care in a skilled nursing facility.

Jeannie currently has only $3,000 in her checking account. She receives $700 per month in gross Social Security, $1,200 per month in gross Civil Service pension benefits, and $200 per month in gross monthly survivor benefit pay from United States Army (as part of a benefit she receives from her deceased combat veteran husband). Jeannie's total gross monthly income is $2,100.

Jeannie will need a Qualified Income Trust to qualify for Medicaid benefits. Jeannie's oldest daughter Christina is currently serving as Jeannie's attorney-in-fact under a durable power of attorney prepared by Jeannie's longtime family lawyer. The durable power of attorney is properly drafted and executed, and the durable power of attorney contains a provision in the document which gives the attorney-in-fact authority to establish a Qualified Income Trust.

Jeannie's income sources have the following deductions: $99.90 is deducted every month from Jeannie's Social Security, and $200 is deducted every month from Jeannie's Civil Service pension for Federal income taxes. There are no other deductions.

Christina has retained an attorney who practices in elder law, and the attorney drafted a Qualified Income Trust titled, "Jeannie Smith Income-Only Trust." Christina executes the Qualified Income-Only Trust at the lawyer's office on behalf of her mother, acting as her mother's attorney-in-fact.

Christina's lawyer applies for an employer identification number (EIN) over the phone with the Internal Revenue Service. Christina then takes the original Qualified Income Trust and the EIN to the bank, where Jeannie maintains her existing checking account.

The bank teller opens a new checking account in the name of "Jeannie Smith Income-Only Trust" under the employer identification number. The bank teller then deposits $2,100 into the new Qualified Income Trust checking account, with the money from Jeannie's existing checking account. The new Qualified Income-Only Trust has now been properly funded.

Jeannie's existing checking account now has only $900 left in it. The process of funding the income trust also brings Jeannie below her allowable $2,000 asset limit for countable assets. Once Jeannie's income has been transferred into the Qualified Income Trust checking account, the state no longer views the $2,100 in the Qualified Income Trust as a countable asset. Jeannie now meets all requirements for Medicaid benefits.

CHAPTER 3

The Three Medicaid Programs for Nursing Homes and Assisted Living Facilities

This chapter reviews the three primary Medicaid programs available in Florida for skilled nursing facilities and assisted living facilities. Although there are significant differences between each of these three programs, each program requires that the Medicaid applicant meet the criteria of the three-part test – health care, assets and income.

The three programs are:

- The Institutional Care Program, for skilled nursing facilities
- The Medicaid Waiver
- The Long Term Care Diversion Program for assisted living facilities

The Institutional Care Program (ICP)

The Institutional Care Program is the primary Medicaid program for elderly and disabled individuals who need long-term care in a skilled nursing facility. ICP pays for the cost of care for the nursing home resident, minus the Medicaid recipient's patient responsibility. ICP has the three basic requirements for Medicaid qualification, as discussed in Chapter 2:

- The Health Care Test
- The Asset Test
- The Income Test

As a general rule, an ICP applicant must be 65 years or older — or, if under 65, classified as disabled. An ICP applicant also needs to be a US citizen, or an otherwise legally qualified resident alien. The ICP applicant must also be classified as a Florida resident.

Once a Medicaid applicant is approved for Medicaid, the cost of the facility for a single person will be his or her gross income, minus $35 personal needs allowance, minus the cost of any secondary health insurance premium.

Example: Lilian is an 87-year-old resident of Osceola County, Florida. She suffers from advanced dementia, and she has recently been admitted to a nursing home. Her doctor has recommended long-term care in a skilled nursing facility.

Lilian is widowed, and she receives $570 per month in gross Social Security. She has an $800 balance in her checking account. She has no private health insurance. After she is approved for ICP Medicaid, Lilian's monthly patient responsibility at the nursing home will be $570, minus her $35 personal needs allowance, for a total of $535.

The private pay rate at the nursing home is $200 per day, or approximately $6,000 per month.

Qualifying for Medicaid will save Lilian and her family over $5,000 per month. In addition to the substantial cost savings at the nursing home, Medicaid will pay for all of her prescription medications, hospitalization, outpatient medical care, counseling, most inpatient and outpatient medical treatments, medical supplies, over-the-counter medications, and transportation to and from doctor's offices and hospitals. There can also be coverage for hearing aids, eyeglasses, and dental care.

The Medicaid Waiver Program for Assisted Living Facilities (Medicaid Waiver)

The Medicaid Waiver Program for Assisted Living Facilities (ALF) has similar requirements to the Medicaid Institutional Care Program. As with ICP Medicaid, there are three basic tests:

- The Health Care Test
- The Asset Test
- The Income Test

As a general rule, a Medicaid Waiver applicant must be 60 or older but, as with ICP Medicaid, there can be exceptions to this general rule. However, there tends to be an extremely long waiting list for Medicaid Waiver applicants who are under the age of 60. As with ICP Medicaid, the health care test is verified by the Florida Department of Elder Affairs CARES Unit. The asset and income tests are verified by the Adult Services Unit of the Florida Department of Children and Families.

One of the reasons for the Medicaid Waiver Program is that it enables assisted living residents who meet the three criteria for Medicaid to remain in a less restrictive environment (and less costly for the State of Florida). It serves as an alternative to the often hospital-like setting of a skilled nursing facility. The Medicaid Waiver Program pays for care similar to the ICP Medicaid. Medications, and most medical treatments, either as an inpatient or as an outpatient, are generally covered.

Example: Betty is an 83-year-old widow who has been living in the same assisted living facility for four years. Betty has dementia, and she needs assistance with most of the ADLs.

Betty has spent most of her life savings on the ALF. She

was not aware that she could have potentially been qualified for Medicaid years earlier by using legal asset-protection strategies that have been available in Florida.

The ALF accepts only the Medicaid Waiver Program.

Betty only has $1,800 left in her checking account, and she receives $900 per month in gross Social Security money.

If she passes the health care test, and after she has been evaluated by the Department of Elder Affairs CARES Unit, she will meet the three criteria for the Medicaid Waiver Program.

After being approved for the Medicaid Waiver Program, the cost of facility (Betty's patient responsibility) will equal $900 minus $54, or $846 per month. The Medicaid Waiver Program will cover most costs associated with Betty's health care needs, including medications.

Coverage under the Medicaid Waiver Program is generally very good for the Medicaid recipient; however, relatively few assisted living facilities take part in the Medicaid Waiver Program. As a result, the selection choices among facilities tend to be somewhat limited. The primary reason for such low participation in the Medicaid Waiver Program by assisted living facilities appears to be the comparatively low reimbursement rates provided from the government.

The Long Term Care Diversion Medicaid Program (Medicaid Diversion)

The Long Term Care Diversion Medicaid Program is a special type of Medicaid Waiver Program. This program incorporates the use of managed care health insurance companies to deliver services to assisted living residents (as well as to individuals living in the community). The Medicaid Diversion Program also has the same basic requirements for qualification as ICP Medicaid and the Medicaid Waiver Program:

- The Health Care Test
- The Asset Test
- The Income Test

The Medicaid Diversion Program applies only to individuals who are 65 or older. The health care coverage provided under the Medicaid Diversion Program is similar to the coverage provided by ICP Medicaid and the Medicaid Waiver Programs.

There are some important differences between Medicaid Diversion, Medicaid Waiver, and ICP Medicaid. To generalize, ICP Medicaid and the Medicaid Waiver Program can be seen as very comparable programs. However, Medicaid Diversion has some significant differences, when compared with both ICP Medicaid and Medicaid Waiver. The differences include:

The Health Care Test. The health care test for the Medicaid Diversion Program is generally more difficult to pass, when compared with ICP Medicaid and Medicaid Waiver. To medically qualify for Medicaid Diversion, the Medicaid applicant must require assistance with a higher number of the Activities of Daily Living (ADLs). The result is that a person might qualify medically for ICP Medicaid – but not for the Medicaid Diversion Program. This makes no sense, because skilled nursing facilities provide a higher level of skilled medical care than assisted living facilities.

Example: Henry is 92 years old, and he has relatively severe dementia. Even though Henry has severe memory problems because of his dementia, he is in very good physical health, and he needs no assistance with the activities of daily living.

Henry has been living in an assisted living facility that accepts the Medicaid Diversion Program.

Henry has spent all of his assets on the assisted living facility, and he can no longer afford to pay privately for the facility.

Because Henry needs no assistance with the ADL's, Henry likely would not qualify medically for the Medicaid Diversion Program.

Henry's only options at this time would be to move to a

facility that accepts Medicaid Waiver, or move to a nursing facility that accepts ICP Medicaid.

Henry would be much more likely to qualify for Medicaid Waiver or ICP Medicaid under these circumstances.

As Henry's case shows, Medicaid (through CARES) may deny a Medicaid applicant to Medicaid Diversion for failing the health care test — even though *financially* qualified for Medicaid assistance. Because of a situation such as Henry's, a CARES evaluation should be done *before* the applicant takes steps to have his assets restructured under the Medicaid Diversion Program.

How the Care Is Provided. The Long Term Care Diversion Program is a Medicaid program that is administered through managed care health insurance companies. (This is very different from Medicaid Waiver and ICP Medicaid, which are administered directly through the State of Florida.) Some of the more popular Long Term Care Diversion providers are:

1. American Elder Care
2. Amerigroup
3. Neighborly Care Network
4. Tango Plan
5. Evercare
6. United Home Care
7. Universal Health Care

During the Medicaid application process, an applicant must complete a "Freedom of Choice" form. On the form, the applicant must select one of the long-term care diversion providers that offers a contract at the assisted living facility of his or her choice. The assisted living facilities that accept Medicaid Diversion will have a contract with one or more of the long-term care providers. The Medicaid applicant (or his/her representative) will, therefore, need to ask the assisted living facility about which long-term care diversion providers with which the facility has a contract.

The Number of Available Facilities. More assisted living facilities accept the Medicaid Diversion Program than the Medicaid Waiver Program. As discussed earlier, the primary reason for this difference appears to be an issue of reimbursement to the facility by the state. The reimbursement rates to assisted living facilities that accept the Medicaid Diversion Program is generally higher than the reimbursement rates to assisted living facilities under the Medicaid Waiver Program.

Patient Responsibility. The calculation of patient responsibility is significantly different for the Long Term Care Diversion Program. The ICP Medicaid Program and the Medicaid Waiver Program both have fairly simple calculations to determine patient responsibility. Determining patient responsibility for the Medicaid Diversion Program depends on several factors. The first has to do with the terms of the contract that the assisted living facility has with the managed care health insurance companies. The amount paid by the long-term care diversion provider generally ranges between $1,000 to $1,400 per month, depending on which insurance company is involved.

Another difference in the Medicaid patient responsibility has to do with monthly income. If a Medicaid applicant's income is relatively high, the Medicaid applicant may have extra funds left over each month to buy personal items.

If, however, the Medicaid applicant's income is comparatively low, his or her family may actually have to pay an out-of-pocket amount to the assisted living facility each month – after the applicant has qualified for Medicaid. Because of this, low-income applicants may prefer to seek placement in either a Medicaid Waiver facility or a skilled nursing facility.

Example: Rosalinda is 94 years old, and she is a resident of Pasco County, Florida.

She receives $230 per month in gross monthly income, has less than $2,000 in her checking account, and this is the only asset she owns.

The CARES Unit has completed a medical assessment of Rosalinda, and they have determined that she passed the strict health care test for the Medicaid Diversion Program.

Rosalinda's family has arranged for Rosalinda to be placed at a very nice Long Term Care Diversion facility.

After discussions with the business office at the facility, the family was notified that they would have to pay an additional $800 each month, even though Rosalinda was qualified for Medicaid Diversion.

Because Rosalinda's low income had caused an unmanageably large out-of-pocket expense for the family, Rosalinda's family had to place her in a facility that accepted Medicaid Waiver.

After placement in the new Medicaid Waiver facility, the patient responsibility for Rosalinda each month was only $176 per month (her $230 gross income minus her $54 personal needs allowance).

CHAPTER 4

How Single People
Can Protect Their Assets

From reading the previous chapter, you might conclude that the only people who can qualify for Medicaid in Florida are unfortunate individuals who are broke (or nearly so). However, even people who have significant assets can qualify.

There are several proven strategies available to help nursing home and assisted living residents both protect their assets and also receive Medicaid benefits. *It is important to note that asset protection does not mean you are cheating the government.* The government itself has made possible these asset protection strategies, and they work for ICP Medicaid, the Medicaid Waiver Program and the Medicaid Diversion Program. These strategies include:

- The Personal Services Contract
- A Special Needs Pooled Trust
- Medicaid Qualifying Annuities
- Purchase of Income Producing Property

- Purchase of a Homestead
- Gifting
- Purchase of Other Exempt Assets
- Repairs to the Homestead
- Payment of Debts and Expenses

Personal Services Contract

A Personal Services Contract is an effective way to reduce the countable assets of a Medicaid applicant. Florida law allows for a reasonable dollar amount to be paid to one or more caregivers involved in the care of the Medicaid applicant. The caregivers must work under a written, properly drafted, and properly executed personal services contract.

Frequently, the individual who acts as the attorney-in-fact, or the guardian of the Medicaid applicant, has spent a significant amount of time involved in the care of the individual. A personal services contract allows for a lump-sum payment (or staggered payments, with certain restrictions) for future services to be paid to the caregiver.

Florida case law authorizes the use of "reasonable personal services contracts" to obtain Medicaid benefits.[7] There are several basic requirements for personal service contracts:

1. The contract payment price must be "reasonable," and the payment cannot exceed a "fair market value." The "reasonableness" of the contract payment could vary, depending on the educational and/or formal medical training of the provider. Fair market value cost of service would be evaluated based on the average hourly cost of geriatric case managers in the region where the Medicaid applicant resides.

2. The contract must be a payment for future services, and not a payment for services already provided.

3. The term of the contract must be equal to or less than the Medicaid applicant's life expectancy, based on actuarial tables

as provided in the *Florida Economic Self-Sufficiency Public Assistance Policy Manual.*[8]

4. The contract must be in writing.

The caregiver will need to remember that any money they are paid from work done under a Personal Services Contract must be counted as "gross income."[9] The caregiver must pay taxes on income earned from a Personal Services Contract when his or her taxes are filed. To learn the amount of tax that will have to be paid, a caregiver may require the help of a tax professional.

Example: Judith is an 82-year-old resident of Panama City, Florida. Her doctor has determined that Judith needs long-term care in a nursing home.

Judith has $31,000 in her checking account – Judith's only asset.

Judith's daughter and attorney-in-fact, Sandra, has hired an elder law attorney to obtain Medicaid benefits for Judith under the ICP Medicaid Program. Sandra's two sisters, Julia and Stephanie, are also involved in the care of their mother.

The elder law attorney prepares a $30,000 personal services contract, with three $10,000 checks payable to Sandra, Julia and Stephanie. The contract is signed by each daughter, and Sandra signs for her mother (acting as her mother's attorney-in-fact). The $30,000 in payments reduces Judith's checking account to $1,000, which is below the allowable $2,000 cash asset limit.

Assuming that Judith meets the two other requirements for Medicaid, Judith will qualify for Medicaid assistance. Each of the three daughters will be paid for services they will perform, and they now have an additional $10,000 of gross income to report on their income tax returns for the year in which the money was paid.

Caregiver relatives, such as Judith's daughters, might also be the beneficiaries of the Medicaid applicant's estate. However, if the caregiver is not a beneficiary of the Medicaid applicant's estate, there is the potential for conflict. For example, if the Medicaid applicant were to die early into the term of a Personal Services Contract, beneficiaries who were not paid under the personal services contract would be left with essentially nothing to inherit.

Special Needs Pooled Trust (Pooled Trust)

A Special Needs Pooled Trust is an effective way for a Medicaid applicant to shelter assets and immediately obtain Medicaid benefits. A Pooled Trust is an irrevocable trust, authorized by the Omnibus Budget Reconciliation Act of 1993.[10]

Most trusts are unable to protect assets held in the trust from the Medicaid "spend-down." For example, many Florida residents have Revocable Living Trusts. A Revocable Living Trust is an estate-planning document, which, if properly established, avoids the probate process after a person dies. However, assets held inside a Revocable Living Trust will be treated as countable assets by Medicaid. Therefore, a Revocable Living Trust will provide no value in terms of helping an applicant qualify for Medicaid benefits.

Florida has adopted the federal law for Pooled Trusts in the *Florida Economic Self-Sufficiency Public Assistance Policy Manual*.[11] There are several basic requirements for a Pooled Trust:

1. A nonprofit association must manage and establish the trust. (The trustee is typically a nonprofit "501(c)(3)" organization.)
2. Each trust beneficiary has his/her own subaccount, but the funds must be managed and invested together.
3. Each individual's subaccount is established for the sole benefit of the person applying for or currently receiving public benefits (Medicaid).

4. Upon the death of the public benefits recipient, the funds held in his/her account will either be required to remain in the Pooled Trust, or to be paid as reimbursement to the state, for the public benefits paid out.

Those requirements may seem stiff, but the Pooled Trust offers several advantages. First, the funds are available to pay for the supplemental needs of the Medicaid recipient. The funds can be used for anything that benefits the Medicaid recipient. This includes payments for a private room at the facility, repairs or costs associated with a homestead still owned by the Medicaid recipient, attorneys fee's, guardianship fee's, etc.

The Pooled Trust funds cannot, however, be paid directly to the Medicaid recipient; instead, payments must be made directly to a service provider or a vendor. By using a Pooled Trust, the beneficiary is now a recipient of public benefits, there will be no spend-down of the beneficiary's assets, and the Medicaid recipient's assets will last much longer.

One big drawback of the Pooled Trust is that the assets held in the Pooled Trust generally will not be inherited by the beneficiaries of the Medicaid recipient's estate. The law requires a payback (for benefits paid out) to the State of Florida of any funds that remain in the trust at the time of the Medicaid recipient's death. Or, if there are other participants in the "pool," the funds may remain in the Pooled Trust after the death of the Medicaid recipient, for the benefit of other participants.

Example: Mary, a 95-year-old resident of Polk County, Florida, has $120,000 in her checking account, and she is widowed with no children. Mary has no other assets, and she has been renting at an independent living facility for the past few years.

Mary has recently fallen and broken her pelvis. Her doctor is now recommending long-term care for Mary at a skilled nursing facility. The nursing facility charges approximately $6,000 per month.

Mary's great-niece, Joyce, is Mary's attorney-in-fact. Joyce contacts an elder law attorney regarding the situation. Mary and Joyce decide, after discussion with the attorney, that Mary should use the Pooled Trust option. Mary decides to have all of her money, except for $1,700 in her regular checking account, to be held in the Pooled Trust.

Mary's gross monthly income from Social Security is $500, and she has no health insurance. Mary's attorney applies for Medicaid, and Mary obtains Medicaid benefits with a patient responsibility of $465 per month. Medicaid pays for the nursing facility, which results in a savings of over $5,000 per month.

Mary will be able to have payments made on her behalf out of the Pooled Trust, and her funds will probably last her the rest of her life. She can also authorize payments to her great-niece, Joyce, over the years, for the time Joyce will contribute to the care of Mary in the future.

A Pooled Trust is often an ideal way to obtain Medicaid benefits for an elderly individual who has no children. It is also used by a Medicaid applicant who is not overly concerned about leaving money to specific people after the Medicaid applicant's death.

Further, if the Medicaid recipient has a desire for his or her funds to be used for the benefit of other disabled or elderly individuals after he or she dies, the Pooled Trust is a good option to consider. The funds that remain in the trust, after the Medicaid recipient dies, can be used for the benefit of the other surviving participants in the Pooled Trust.

Medicaid Qualifying Annuity

A Medicaid Qualifying Annuity is a specially structured annuity that meets the following criteria:

- No cash value
- Non-assignable

- Non-transferable
- Single premium immediate annuity
- Term of the annuity is equal to or less than life expectancy under the Social Security life expectancy tables

If these requirements are met, then this type of annuity will work to restructure countable assets into non-countable assets. Florida law also requires the annuity to pay out a certain dollar amount on a monthly basis, which would be paid to the nursing facility as part of a single Medicaid applicant's patient responsibility.

The Deficit Reduction Act of 2005 (DRA), to be discussed in detail in a Chapter 6, requires that the State of Florida be named as the primary beneficiary of the annuity (to the extent of Medicaid benefits paid out). The DRA requires that all Medicaid annuities for single Medicaid applicants be "level payout" annuities. This means there is no "balloon" payment (a large, lump-sum payment scheduled at the end of the smaller, periodic payments). All payments are equal in amount.

Example: Cecelia is an 87-year-old widow who has a $61,000 balance in her checking account, and she receives $800 per month in gross Social Security.

Cecelia is a resident of Merritt Island, Florida, and her physician has determined that she needs long-term care in a skilled nursing facility.

Cecelia has two children, Tom and Katie. Tom is Cecelia's attorney-in-fact. Tom retains an elder law attorney to assist the family in obtaining Medicaid benefits for Cecelia.

After consideration of the various options, the family decides to use a level payout Medicaid qualifying annuity. The attorney has referred the family to an insurance agent who specializes in Medicaid qualifying annuities. The family establishes a $60,000 Medicaid qualifying annuity. The state of Florida must be named the primary beneficiary to the extent of Medicaid benefits paid on behalf of Cecelia, which Florida law requires. Tom and Katie are named as secondary beneficiaries, after the state of Florida is paid back Medicaid benefits.

Cecelia's life expectancy is 5.78 years under the Social Security life expectancy tables, and the family decides to set a five-year term for the annuity. The annuity will pay $1,000, per month, over the next 60 months. This amount must be paid to the nursing home each month. Cecelia will now qualify for Medicaid. She has no health insurance, so her Medicaid patient responsibility will be $1,765 per month ($1,000 + $800 - $35 = $1,765).

The Purchase of Income-Producing Property

The *Florida Economic Self-Sufficiency Public Assistance Policy Manual* provides that real estate rented for fair market value is excluded from a Medicaid applicant's countable resources.[12] The *Policy Manual* also states that only the *net* rent (the gross rent minus expenses) will count toward the Medicaid applicant's patient responsibility.[13]

Expense items that are considered allowable deductions from the rent include:

- property taxes
- property insurance
- repairs
- utilities
- monthly maintenance fees
- interest
- debts

These items would first be deducted from the gross rent amount, and the balance would be paid to the facility.

The *Policy Manual* also requires that the real estate be rented for fair market value. If this strategy were used to restructure assets, then it would be important to include, with the Medicaid application, a letter from a real estate professional stating that the property is indeed rented for fair market value.

Another issue with the use of this strategy relates to what would happen to the property after the death of the Medicaid applicant. When a Medicaid applicant dies, if his or her rental property goes through probate, the State of Florida would then recover against the property to repay Medicaid benefits paid out to the Medicaid recipient during his or her life.

There are two primary ways to avoid probate with real property:

1. The use of an Enhanced Life Estate Deed
2. The use of a Revocable Living Trust

Example: Bernice is a 101-year-old widow and a resident of Palm Beach County, Florida. She has suffered a stroke and she needs long-term placement in a skilled nursing facility.

Bernice has $600,000 in a money market account, her only asset. Bernice receives $1,000 per month in gross Social Security.

Bernice has four children, who are equal beneficiaries of her revocable living trust. Bernice's oldest daughter, Nicole, is Bernice's attorney-in-fact. Bernice's son Gabriel is a professional real estate investor.

Nicole retains an elder law attorney to try to deal with the estimated $7,000 in monthly charges that are expected at the nursing home where Bernice has been placed. After discussing the family's situation, the attorney advises them to consider the purchase of a rental condominium unit near the ocean for approximately $599,000.

A real estate agent has prepared a letter stating that such a condominium should rent for approximately $1,800 per month, with about $500 in expenses per month.

Nicole, using her durable power of attorney, buys a waterfront condominium in the name of her mother's trust (to avoid probate after her mother dies). The condominium is rented for $1,800 per month on a two-year lease to a family that has just relocated to West Palm Beach.

Because the rental income now puts Bernice over the 2012 income cap of $2,094 gross per month, the attorney prepares a Qualified Income Trust. The trust is funded each month with $2,300 from Bernice's monthly income. The nursing facility is paid $2,265. Since the nursing home costs $7,000 per month, nearly $5,000 per month is saved.

Because Bernice's four children are named equal beneficiaries in the Revocable Living Trust, the condominium will bypass probate when Bernice dies. Title to the property will then pass to her four children without any Medicaid benefit recovery (under current law).

If a Medicaid applicant is very elderly (late 90s to over 100 years old) and has significant assets (over $200,000 in countable assets) that need to be restructured to protect them from Medicaid, the use of rental real estate as a restructuring option becomes a good option because:

- A person over 100 years old is generally considered uninsurable, so an annuity strategy would not be an option.

- The dollar amount of a personal services contract would be restricted by the short life expectancy of the Medicaid applicant.

Therefore, a very elderly person with substantial assets often presents the ideal scenario for sheltering assets with a real estate rental strategy.

One issue that might make investing in rental real estate undesirable relates to the property management and landlord/tenant issues. Property management is often a difficult and time-consuming undertaking. If a close family member of the Medicaid applicant is involved in real estate investment, such as Bernice's son Gabriel, a real estate investment strategy often makes sense. A professional property manager can also be hired to manage the property, and up to 10% of the monthly rent could be paid to the property manager, and deducted from the patient responsibility.

The Purchase of a Homestead

A Medicaid applicant is allowed to have one home in Florida, with a $525,000 limit on the value. The home can be a house, a mobile home, a condominium or any other place the Medicaid applicant lives, and which he or she owns.

For the homestead to be considered an exempt asset, the Medicaid applicant must have an "intent" to return home, which seems to be generally presumed by most DCF caseworkers. Simply because a Medicaid applicant lives in a nursing home, or in an assisted living facility, does not mean that they don't intend to one day go home.

"Intent" is a psychological state of mind, and it has nothing to do with a Medicaid applicant's *physical* inability to return home.

The Deficit Reduction Act has established a $500,000 (adjusted in 2012 to $525,000) upper value limit, or cap, on home equity for unmarried Medicaid applicants. If a spouse is still living at home, the equity cap does not apply. (This aspect of the Deficit Reduction Act will be discussed in the Chapter 6.)

In addition to having the "intent" to return home, the Medicaid applicant must have actually physically lived at the home at some time in the past. If the Medicaid applicant never actually resided in the home, the DCF case worker could conceivably take the position that there was no "intent" to return home, since they never actually lived in the home to begin with. For that reason, a prospective Medicaid applicant who is *already* a permanent resident in a nursing home or an assisted living facility may not find the purchase of a homestead a viable strategy to shelter assets. The purchase of income producing property would be the preferred option, if the Medicaid applicant already resides in a nursing home or an assisted living facility and does not currently own a home.

> **Example:** Esmeralda is an 89-year-old widow who lives at home in Hobe Sound, Florida. In recent years, she has experienced various health problems, but she is still capable of living at home. Esmeralda's doctor has indicated that Esmeralda may need assisted living care — within the next two years.
>
> Her daughter and power of attorney, Daniela, has arranged for a geriatric care manager to spend five hours per week to visit Esmeralda at her home.
>
> Esmeralda's house is a small, two-bedroom house worth approximately $120,000. Esmeralda also has $280,000 in bank accounts and other liquid investments.
>
> It would be perfectly acceptable under the Medicaid rules for Esmeralda to sell her current home and move into a home worth significantly more, and thereby reduce her countable assets. As long as Esmeralda actually resides in her new home, it would be considered exempt under Florida law if she later needed to apply for Medicaid benefits in a nursing home or assisted living facility (which her doctor anticipates will be the case within two years).

Many Florida residents have Revocable Living Trusts for the purpose of avoiding probate. Although the "intent" to return home generally is the controlling factor in determining whether the home is exempt for Medicaid purposes, there are some provisions under federal law that indicate that any assets held in a Revocable Living Trust are "countable" assets for the purpose of obtaining public benefits.[14] Because of this, some attorneys advise Medicaid applicants, who own their homestead in a living trust, to quitclaim the homestead out of the trust and back into the name of the Medicaid applicant (and any spouse if there is a spouse) before applying for Medicaid. But the Department of Children and Families uses the "intent to return home" policy to decide whether the home is exempt for purposes of obtaining Medicaid benefits. Therefore, it is not necessary to transfer the homestead out of the Revocable Living Trust to obtain Medicaid benefits.

Gifting (Asset Transfers for Less than Fair Market Value)

There are strict limitations on gifting, when it comes to Medicaid planning. The general rule under Federal and Florida law is that individuals are largely prohibited from giving away assets to obtain Medicaid benefits. The Florida Department of Children and Families uses a "divestment penalty divisor" to calculate Medicaid disqualification periods for people who give away assets, and then apply for Medicaid. The current divestment penalty divisor is $5,000, which is the dollar amount that represents the average monthly private pay rate of a skilled nursing facility in Florida. The Florida Department of Children and Families has issued Proposed Rule 65A-1.76, which reflects an increase in the average monthly nursing home private cost. Based on this proposed rule, the penalty divisor will increase from $5,000 to $6,880 sometime during 2012.

It is important to distinguish between Florida Medicaid gifting rules and the gifting rules with regard to the filing of a federal gift tax return (IRS Form 709).[15] Many people confuse the IRS $13,000 annual gift tax exclusion with the Medicaid gifting rules. These two concepts are not related.

> **Example:** Angelica is an 83-year-old widow, and she is a resident of Jacksonville, Florida.
>
> Angelica has a balance of $121,000 in her checking account and no other assets. Angelica receives $1,000 per month in gross Social Security.
>
> Angelica has recently been admitted to a skilled nursing facility.

Angelica has one daughter, Dulce Maria. Angelica gives a $60,000 gift to Dulce Maria, creating a 12-month penalty period for Medicaid. At the same time, Angelica establishes a $60,000, 12-month, level payout annuity, which pays out $5,000 per month for the next year. The $60,000 gift disqualifies Angelica for Medicaid for one year, but the $5,000 monthly annuity, and $1,000 per month in Social Security, pay for the nursing home's $6,000-per-month bill.

Angelica also would need to establish a qualified income trust, because her income would now exceed $2,094 per month. At the end of the 12-month penalty period, Angelica would be qualified for Medicaid, and Angelica would have transferred (and preserved) $60,000 with the gift to Dulce Maria.

Under Section 102 of the Internal Revenue Code, gifts and inheritances are not classified as income. Because of that, any money received as a gift or an inheritance is not reportable to the IRS as income.

The Purchase of Other Exempt Assets

There are a number of other, different types of assets that are exempt from Medicaid. Household items such as furniture, clothing, and appliances are generally going to be considered exempt. (Certain exceptions to that rule would be valuable artwork and certain types of antiques.) Other exempt assets include:

- hearing aids
- eyeglasses
- dentures
- wheelchairs
- personal computers
- televisions
- one automobile

- up to $2,500 in a burial savings account per spouse
- an unlimited amount for an irrevocable funeral or cremation contract for each spouse.

If any of these items would be of value to a Medicaid applicant (or his or her spouse), it is often advisable to consider buying them to reduce countable assets.

Example: Carlo is a 95-year-old widower who has been permanently admitted to a nursing home in Florida.

Carlo has $5,000 in his checking account.

Carlo needs to qualify for Medicaid immediately.

Carlo needs new dentures, and he recently lost his hearing aids.

If Carlo were to spend $1,500 on new hearing aids, and open a $2,000 burial savings account, he would bring his checking account below $2,000, and he would be immediately qualified for Medicaid.

Repairs to the Homestead

Making repairs to an existing homestead is often a good way to reduce countable assets. Permissible repairs or upgrades to the homestead include:

- painting
- roofing
- installation of new carpet
- the purchase of new furniture and appliances
- installation of new counter tops and cabinets
- upgrading plumbing, electrical work and landscaping

Example: Soledad is a 78-year-old widow confined to a nursing home in Florida, and she will need to stay permanently in the facility due to her serious health problems.

Soledad has $20,000 in her checking account.

Soledad's home is 50 years old and is worth $200,000. The house still has the original roof, which leaks when it rains.

If Soledad buys a new roof for her house for $19,000, this brings her countable asset limit below $2,000, and she will be immediately qualified for Medicaid.

Payment of Debts and Expenses

If a Medicaid applicant has a mortgage, car loan, credit card bills, or any other debts, paying these debts is often a good strategy to shelter countable monies.

Example: Alma is 91 years old and permanently confined to a skilled nursing facility in Deland, Florida.

Alma has a $200,000 home and $83,000 in her checking account, her only assets. There is $82,000 worth of debt on the house.

If Alma were to pay off the balance of the mortgage with the money in her checking account, it would reduce her countable assets to below $2,000, and Alma would become immediately qualified for Medicaid.

CHAPTER 5

Additional Ways
Married Individuals
Can Protect Their Assets

The asset protection strategies discussed in Chapter 4, regarding asset protection for single individuals, will also apply for married individuals. However, there are additional methods available for married couples when one spouse is confined to a nursing home and the other spouse still lives in the community.

Under current law, if one spouse is applying for Medicaid and one spouse is going to remain at home, the spouse applying for Medicaid is allowed to have no more than $2,000 in countable assets. The spouse still living at home (called the "community" spouse) is allowed to have no more than $113,640 in countable assets in 2012. If both spouses need to apply for Medicaid benefits in a facility, then both spouses are allowed to have no more that $3,000 in combined, countable assets.

When a married person applies for Medicaid, the income test applies to only the spouse who is applying for Medicaid benefits, and additional planning opportunities are created.

The Medicaid Qualifying Annuity

The Medicaid Qualifying Annuity, discussed in Chapter 4, has no cash value. It is an irrevocable, non-assignable, non-transferable, single-premium, immediate annuity. The term of annuity is equal to or less than life expectancy (under the Social Security life expectancy tables).

The community spouse, however, is not subject to the income cap, and there is no patient responsibility for the community spouse. It sometimes makes sense to set up an annuity that is owned by the community spouse — an annuity that has a very high monthly income payout.

To accomplish a high monthly income payout, a "level payout" Medicaid Qualifying Annuity can be used if it meets all the basic requirements of a Medicaid Qualifying Annuity and pays income to the community spouse each month. Such an annuity will not affect the institutionalized spouse's Medicaid eligibility. Under the Deficit Reduction Act, the primary beneficiary is the State of Florida, to repay Medicaid benefits paid out on behalf of the Medicaid recipient.

Example: Antonio is an 85-year-old man, married to 82-year-old Lisette. They are residents of Miami, Florida.

Antonio recently suffered a stroke, and he is currently in the hospital awaiting discharge to a skilled nursing facility. Antonio's doctor has recommended that Antonio remain in the nursing home for long-term care.

Antonio has $1,500 in his checking account, Lisette has $160,000 in a money market account, and they own a home and one car together.

Because of the $160,000 in Lisette's money market account, Lisette exceeds her 2012 countable asset limit of $113,640. At age 82, Lisette's life expectancy is 8.21 years (under the Social Security life expectancy tables). If Lisette were to purchase a four-year, level-payout Medicaid Qualifying Annuity for $60,000 — which would pay her $1,250 per month over the next four years – Antonio would immediately qualify for Medicaid. There would be no Medicaid spend-down, and Lisette would receive the entire annuity principal back in the form of monthly payments over the next four years.

Spousal Refusal *or* Assignment of Rights to Support

Another option available to obtain Medicaid benefits for married couples is called "spousal refusal" or "assignment of rights to support." Spousal refusal is a legal strategy available in Florida whereby a married couple can obtain Medicaid benefits for one spouse. Countable assets, in excess of $2,000, are transferred to the healthy spouse. After the countable assets (in excess of $2,000) have been transferred, the healthy spouse then "refuses" to make his/her assets available to pay to the nursing home. If the community spouse exceeds his/her $113,640 in countable assets limit for 2012, spousal refusal is another way to quickly obtain Medicaid benefits.[16]

Spousal refusal will only work if *only one* spouse is applying for Medicaid benefits. There is a specific Florida form ("Assignment of Rights to Support") that needs to be signed by the spouse who applies for Medicaid, and a statement that also needs to be signed by the community spouse. Under the spousal refusal strategy, there is effectively no asset limit for the community spouse. The risk of using a spousal refusal strategy is that the State of Florida maintains the right to recover Medicaid benefits paid out (from the community spouse).

Florida has never pursued recovery of benefits under this strategy, which may be because:

1. If the State of Florida were to recover benefits, any recovery would have to be shared with the federal government.

2. There may be legal barriers restricting the State of Florida from recovering against the community spouse under Florida law.[17]

3. It may not be politically popular to take legal action against elderly Florida community spouses.

4. Relatively few people know about the spousal refusal strategy, so it is rarely used, and it therefore does not have a significant impact on Florida's Medicaid budget.

5. The majority of nursing home and assisted living facility applicants are unmarried, and the spousal refusal strategy is available only to married medicaid applicants.

Example: Jack is 89 years old, and his wife Madeline is 84 years old. Jack and Madeline are residents of Orange County, Florida.

Jack has recently undergone surgery to repair a hip he injured many years ago, during his well-known career as a circus acrobat. Unfortunately, the surgery to his hip has triggered relatively severe dementia. Jack's doctor is now recommending long-term care in a skilled nursing facility for Jack.

Jack and Madeline retired to Florida from New Jersey in 1985, and they own a house in Orange County, Florida, worth $300,000. Jack has a checking account with a balance of $1,500; Madeline has a checking account with a balance $30,000. Madeline previously inherited a house from her parents in Tenafly, New Jersey, which, due to its close proximity to New York City, is now worth $800,000.

Madeline does not want to sell the house in New Jersey to pay for Jack's care. The home has been owned by her family for several generations, and Madeline wants to pass the New Jersey home to her children when Jack and Madeline pass away. With $30,000 in her checking account, Madeline knows that all of her liquid savings will be paid to the nursing home unless she acts quickly.

Madeline hires an attorney who has successfully used the spousal refusal strategy. The attorney recommends that Madeline consider the spousal refusal option. The attorney prepares the proper spousal refusal forms, and submits the Medicaid file to DCF. Jack is approved for Medicaid because his countable assets are below $2,000, and Madeline's house in New Jersey is no longer considered a countable asset because of the spousal refusal strategy.

CHAPTER 6

The Deficit Reduction Act of 2005 (DRA) in Florida

The federal Deficit Reduction Act of 2005 was enacted into law in Florida as part of the Florida Administrative Code (FAC) on November 1, 2007.[18] There are some significant differences between the federal provisions signed into law by President Bush on February 8, 2006, and the version of the law that Florida adopted.[19]

Some of the more important features of the DRA in Florida include the following:

- Long-Term Care Insurance
- Asset Transfer Look-Back Period
- Annuities
- Individual Retirement Accounts (IRAs)
- Gifting (Asset Transfers for Less than Fair Market Value)
- Promissory Notes, Loans and Mortgages
- Life Estates

- Penalty Periods for Gifts
- The "Income First" Rule
- Hardship Claims
- The Homestead Equity Cap
- Entrance Fees for CCRCs or Life Care Communities

Long-Term Care Insurance

The purchase of a qualifying long-term care insurance policy allows for a "resource disregard" in terms of Medicaid qualification. This means that a person with such a long-term care policy will be allowed to keep countable assets with a value equal to the value of the long-term policy and still become eligible for Medicaid benefits.[20]

> **Example:** Ethel, a single Florida resident, purchased a long-term care policy with a $300,000 policy benefit. If Ethel ever needs Medicaid, she will be able to keep $300,000 in countable assets and still qualify for Medicaid benefits.

Asset Transfer Look-Back Period

Florida adopted a 60-month look-back on January 1, 2010. Despite the language of the DRA, the look-back remained 36 months between November 1, 2007 and January 1, 2010.[21] This means that Medicaid will "look back" into an applicant's finances five years (60 months) prior to the date of application.

> **Example:** Floyd, a resident of Putnam County, Florida gave a $10,000 gift to his only daughter, Maggie, in December 2007, leaving Floyd with $1,500 in his checking account. Floyd had heard that a person can have no more than $2,000 for Medicaid, so he thought giving the money away would be a good idea.
>
> In February 2008, Floyd suffered a stroke, and subsequently

required long-term care in a nursing home. Although Floyd had less than $2,000 in February, Floyd's Medicaid application was denied because of the $10,000 gift in December 2007. Florida law states that gifts (for gifts given after November 1, 2007) create a penalty period for Medicaid.

The penalty periods, measured in monthly stages, are figured by dividing the total value of the transferred asset amount by the average monthly rate for a private pay nursing facility. In Florida, the average monthly amount for nursing homes is $5,000, and is designated as the "Divestment Penalty Divisor." The penalty period does not begin to run until the Medicaid application is filed.

Floyd's Medicaid benefits are denied solely because of the gift.

Floyd will become eligible for Medicaid two months after the Medicaid application was denied ($10,000 ÷ $5,000 = 2 months), and Maggie will have to use the money that was gifted to her to pay the nursing home.

Irrevocable Medicaid Five Year Asset Protection Trust

An Irrevocable Medicaid Five Year Asset Protection Trust can be a good option to consider as a Medicaid pre-planning strategy. Under the current Medicaid rules, there is a 60 month (five year) look-back period for transfers to a trust. If one does not expect to need nursing home or assisted living care for a number of years, one might consider transferring assets into an irrevocable trust to reduce countable assets. If the irrevocable trust is properly established, after a five year waiting period, the assets held in the trust will no longer be considered as countable assets. One of the problems with use of this type of trust is that if the person needs Medicaid within five years of transferring the assets to the trust, the person will not be eligible for Medicaid until the end of the five year period. Another problem is that once the assets are transferred into the trust, the assets are now owned by the trust, and the person has in effect given away the assets to the irrevocable trust. Despite these drawbacks, if nursing home or assisted living Medicaid is not expected to be on the horizon for at least five years, the use of an irrevocable trust as a Medicaid pre-planning strategy might be a good option to consider. If skilled nursing home or assisted living care is expected to be needed within five years, then one must seriously consider whether or not an irrevocable trust is an appropriate Medicaid planning strategy for one's particular situation.

Annuities

The DRA requires that Medicaid applicants and their spouses must disclose any annuities that they own.[22] As discussed in Chapter 4, a Medicaid Qualifying Annuity had been a very popular strategy used to help people restructure assets so they can qualify for Medicaid benefits.

In accordance with the Florida version of the DRA, balloon annuities are prohibited for single Medicaid applicants after November 1, 2007. If an annuity is used to shelter countable assets for a single Medicaid applicant, the annuity must be a "level payout" annuity, and all existing criteria for Medicaid Qualifying Annuities must be met (see Chapter 4). With a "level payout" annuity, the entire annuity principal is paid back to the annuitant in equal monthly payments until the entire principal is paid back.

Further, the State of Florida must be named as the primary beneficiary to be reimbursed for Medicaid benefits that were paid out to the Medicaid recipient.

> **Example:** Cecelia is an 87-year-old widow who has a $61,000 balance in her checking account, and she receives $800 per month in gross Social Security.
>
> Cecelia is a resident of Merritt Island, Florida, and her physician has determined that she needs long-term care in a skilled nursing facility.

Cecelia has two children, Tom and Katie. Tom is Cecelia's attorney-in-fact. Tom retains an elder law attorney to assist the family in obtaining Medicaid benefits for Cecelia.

After consideration of the various options, the family decides to use a level payout Medicaid qualifying annuity. The attorney has referred the family to an insurance agent who specializes in Medicaid qualifying annuities. The family establishes a $60,000 Medicaid qualifying annuity. The State of Florida must be named the primary beneficiary to the extent of Medicaid benefits paid on behalf of Cecelia, which Florida law requires. Tom and Katie are named as secondary beneficiaries, after the State of Florida is paid back Medicaid benefits.

Cecelia's life expectancy is 5.78 years under the Social Security life expectancy tables, and the family decides to set a five-year term for the annuity. The annuity will pay $1,000 per month over the next 60 months. This amount must be paid to the nursing home each month.

Cecelia will now qualify for Medicaid. She has no health insurance, so her Medicaid will be $1,765 per month ($1,000 + $800 - $35 = $1,765).

Individual Retirement Accounts (IRAs)

The DRA allows for IRAs to be treated as non-countable assets, as long as the IRA pays out income according to existing Medicaid rules.[23]

Example: Tia is an unmarried, 78-year-old resident of Orange County, Florida.

She owns a $100,000 IRA and has a balance of $1,500 in her regular checking account. These are the only two assets owned by Tia. Tia also receives $400 per month in gross Social Security benefits.

Tia's IRA currently pays a required minimum distribution of

$3,000 in June and December of each year. The IRA is composed of one bank account, which earns $5,000 per year in interest. If Tia changes the payments so that the IRA pays Tia $500 each month, instead of $3,000 every six months, the State of Florida will treat the IRA as an income source only, and not as an asset.

Tia can keep her $100,000 IRA and still qualify for Medicaid — if she changes the IRA payout.

Gifting (Asset Transfers for Less than Fair Market Value)

Gift transfers of assets (or sources of income) for less than fair market value will be deemed to have occurred for the purpose of obtaining Medicaid benefits.[24] However, the Medicaid applicant is given the opportunity to argue and provide evidence that the transfer of assets (or sources of income) was *not* done in an attempt to qualify an applicant for Medicaid benefits.

Example: Abby is an extremely healthy 68-year-old resident of Alachua County, Florida.

Abby's grandchild, Michelle, just started college at the University of Florida. Abby pays $7,000 directly to the University of Florida to pay for Michelle's first semester of college tuition, and room and board.

Three months after the gift, Abby needed long-term care in a nursing home as a result of a car accident. Although the Department of Children and Families will presume that the gift was completed for Medicaid purposes, when Abby later applies for Medicaid it is likely that Abby will be able to rebut that presumption because of the circumstances of the gift.

Promissory Notes, Loans and Mortgages

The DRA allows the use of certain contracts (promissory notes, loans and mortgages) to shelter assets, as long as certain criteria are met.[25] The Florida Department of Children and Families has a preexisting internal memorandum from March 2005, which prohibits the use of promissory notes as a Medicaid planning strategy.[26] However, promissory notes may be an appropriate Medicaid planning strategy under some circumstances.

Life Estates

An ownership interest in a life estate can be a non-countable asset, as long as the Medicaid applicant resides in the property for a minimum of one year.[27]

> **Example:** Lucille is a resident of Nassau County, Florida.
>
> She currently rents a house and has $100,000 in a checking account.
>
> Lucille's lease is about to expire, and she and her daughter Joan have decided that Lucille is going to move into Joan's house. Instead of paying rent, Lucille decides to purchase a life estate in Joan's house, which entitles Lucille to live in Joan's house for the rest of Lucille's life. Lucille pays $99,000 to Joan for the life estate, which is a fair market value price for the life estate, given market conditions.
>
> If Lucille lives in Joan's home for 12 months or more, the $99,000 interest in Joan's home will become an exempt asset for Medicaid purposes.

Penalty Periods for Gifts

Gifts made after November 1, 2007, will be added together so that the gifts will be deemed to have occurred on the date that the Medicaid applicant would have become "otherwise" eligible for Medicaid benefits.[28] This means that the penalty period for gifts will start to run when the applicant applies for Medicaid, and DCF then denies benefits — solely because of the gift.

The new law also provides that there will no longer be any "rounding down" of fractional gift penalty periods.

Under Florida law, prior to November 1, 2007, rounding down of fractional gift penalty periods was permissible. For example, prior to November 2007, if a person gave away $4,900 (slightly less than the $5,000 divestment penalty divisor) a .98 month period of Medicaid disqualification would be created ($5,000 ÷ $4,900 = .98). The State of Florida would round this fraction down to 0 because the fraction was less than 1. A $4,900 gift would thus create 0 months of Medicaid qualification.

Under the new law, however, a $4,900 gift creates .98 months of disqualification for Medicaid, because rounding down of gift fractions is no longer allowed.

The "Income First" Rule

The DRA requires Florida to follow an "Income First" rule, which relates to the minimum monthly maintenance needs allowance for the community spouse.[29] It applies to situations in which the community spouse would want to increase his or her resource (asset) allowance, which is $113,640 in 2012. Under the "income-first" rule, the community spouse can only increase the community spouse resource allowance after all of the nursing-home-resident spouse's income has been diverted to the community spouse.

Example: Isabella and Andrew are residents of Martin County, Florida. Isabella lives in an assisted living facility, which costs

$4,500 per month. Her husband Andrew resides in a skilled nursing facility, which costs $7,000 per month.

Andrew is going to apply for ICP Medicaid benefits. Isabella is going to continue to be a private pay resident at the assisted living facility, because she does not meet the level of care for any of the assisted living Medicaid programs.

The couple owns $140,000 in countable assets, and Isabella receives $2,900 per month in gross monthly income. Andrew receives $800 a month in gross monthly income.

Isabella believes that she will need to keep all of the $140,000 in assets, as well as all of Andrew's monthly income, to pay for the high cost of her care at the assisted living facility. During the Medicaid application process, Isabella could request an appeal to establish that she needs to keep all of the countable assets. (Isabella's countable assets exceed the $113,640 community spouse resource allowance.) Additionally, if Isabella were to receive all of Andrew's income, the total amount would exceed the $2,841 maximum income allocation amount.

An administrative hearing would need to be requested by Isabella regarding both her assets and her income, because what she is requesting exceeds what the law allows, as far as her income and assets are concerned. During the administrative hearing, before Isabella could request a higher resource allowance, she would first need to establish with the hearing officer that if she were to receive all of Andrew's $800 per month in income, that amount would not be sufficient to support Isabella's financial needs.

In other words, Isabella must actually be granted a hearing order whereby she is first authorized to keep **all** of Andrew's income to pay for her expenses before she could request an increase in her resource allowance.

Hardship Claims

New hardship provisions may enable the community spouse or Medicaid applicant to claim hardship to obtain Medicaid benefits.[30] If either spouse can demonstrate "exceptional circumstances" that "result in extreme financial duress," then the limit on allowances available to the community spouse might be increased to remedy the financial duress.

Example: Karen's husband Bruce is currently on ICP Medicaid. Karen receives $1,800 per month in gross Social Security, and Bruce receives $1,000 per month in gross Social Security. Currently, Karen has to pay $965 to the nursing home each month for Bruce's patient responsibility ($1,000 − $35 personal needs allowance).

Karen has severe health problems, and she has no private health insurance. Karen's average monthly doctor's bills and medication bills are $1,500 per month, for herself, which she has to pay out of her own funds. Karen owns a house and a car, but she only has $1,500 in her checking account.

Karen's attorney files a hardship appeal with the Department of Children and Families, because Karen needs the $965 per month, which is currently being paid to the nursing home, to pay her own medical bills.

In a situation such as this, the hearing officer would most likely allow Karen to keep the $965 being paid to the nursing home, decreasing Bruce's patient responsibility to zero, because Karen is under extreme financial duress.

The Homestead Equity Cap

Under the DRA, a $500,000 limit was placed on equity in homestead property (the limit was adjusted to $525,000 in 2012).[31] This provision primarily impacts single Medicaid applicants. This means that a single

Medicaid applicant will not be able to qualify for Medicaid if his or her homestead has over $525,000 in equity. This cap on the homestead does not apply if:

- the spouse of the Medicaid recipient is living at the home
- a child under 21 years is living at the home
- a child who is blind or disabled is living at the home

Entrance Fees for CCRCs or Life Care Communities

The DRA requires Medicaid applicants to count as assets the entrance fees they have paid to continuing care retirement communities (CCRCs) or life care communities.[32]

Example: Walter, an 87-year-old resident of St. Lucie County, Florida, purchased a $50,000 interest in a continuing care retirement community.

Walter has $1,500 in his checking account. Prior to November 1, 2007, the $50,000 entrance fee would have been considered a non-countable asset for Medicaid purposes.

Under the DRA, however, the entrance fee would be considered a countable asset if the following three elements are met:

- Walter has a right to use the entrance fee to pay for his care

- Walter can receive a refund if the contract is terminated (or if Walter's estate could receive a refund)
- If the contract does not result in any ownership interest in the CCRC to Walter

CHAPTER 7

Other Important
Medicaid Planning
Considerations

There are many additional considerations which are relevant to Medicaid planning. Chapter 7 provides an overview of the following legal resources and objectives that can help seniors become eligible for Medicaid benefits, avoid the healthy spouse from becoming impoverished, and preserve their assets:

- Durable power of attorney and guardianship
- Probate avoidance and Medicaid benefit recovery
- Income allocation for the community spouse
- Medicare benefits
- Individual retirement accounts
- Long-term care insurance
- Life estate deeds/enhanced life estate deeds

In addition to these considerations, Veterans benefits can be a significant source of funds for the long-term care needs of elderly and disabled veterans, or their surviving spouses. Veterans benefits are discussed in detail in Chapter 8.

Durable Power of Attorney and Guardianship

Powers of Attorney Executed Before October 1, 2011

As far as Medicaid qualifications are concerned, a properly executed durable power is one of the most important documents in a Medicaid case. A durable power of attorney is a critically important document, because the typical nursing home or assisted living resident is often too ill to act on his or her own behalf. A power of attorney gives another person the legal right to act on someone's behalf. The term "durable" means that the power of attorney document remains in effect even if the principal becomes incapacitated.[33]

In Florida, the power of attorney document must be executed with the same formalities as a real estate deed, which requires the principal (the person who grants the power of attorney) to sign the power of attorney in the presence of a notary public and two impartial witnesses.[34]

A power of attorney is typically most often needed when the principal is incapacitated (either physically or mentally). For this reason, it is critical to establish a valid durable power of attorney *before* a person becomes incapacitated. If a person loses capacity and cannot execute a new durable power of attorney, the only other option is guardianship.

Guardianship is an expensive, time-consuming, court-ordered process. A guardian is appointed by a court to handle the affairs of an incapacitated individual. If there is no durable power of attorney in place, and a guardianship must be established, there can be significant costs and time delays involved in establishing the guardianship.

A delay to complete Medicaid planning happens when a guardianship first has to be established through the court. Additional delays happen when the court has to be petitioned by the guardianship attorney to authorize Medicaid planning. If the Medicaid applicant is already in a nursing facility, the cost will generally be $5,000–$7,000 per month in private pay expenses while the court filings for the guardianship and Medicaid planning authorization are completed. The process can take 3–4 months, depending on the court.

Example 1: Frederik is 85 years old, he has severe dementia and he needs long-term care in a nursing facility.

Frederik has $20,000 in his checking account.

Frederik's son Ralph has a valid durable power of attorney, which was executed when Frederik had capacity to execute the durable power of attorney.

Ralph contacted an attorney knowledgeable in Medicaid planning, and the attorney was able to obtain Medicaid benefits in the same month the attorney was hired.

Frederik's entire estate was preserved.

Example 2: Frederik is 85 years old, he has severe dementia and he needs long-term care in a nursing facility.

Frederik never executed a durable power of attorney when he had capacity.

Frederik has $20,000 in his checking account.

Frederik can no longer execute a new durable power of attorney, because he is now incapacitated.

His son Ralph contacts the same attorney as in Example 1, but now the attorney must establish a guardianship and petition the court to authorize Medicaid planning. Unfortunately, it took three months between the time Ralph originally contacted the attorney until Frederik's Medicaid was authorized.

Because Frederik's facility cost $6,000/month, there is now an $18,000 outstanding bill at the facility, which must be paid from Frederik's $20,000 remaining assets. Because of the length of time it took to establish a guardianship and then obtain court authorization to proceed with Medicaid planning, thousands of dollars were needlessly spent on the nursing home.

Powers of Attorney Executed on or After October 1, 2011

On October 1, 2011, a new power of attorney statute went in to effect in Florida. (Florida Statutes Chapter 709.2101-709.2402). If a Florida power of attorney document was prepared and executed in accordance with Florida law prior to October 1, 2011, then the new statute generally would not affect the previously executed power of attorney. However, for powers of Attorney executed on or after October 1, 2011, the new power of attorney statute would apply. The new power of attorney is a significant change in Florida law. The following are some of the major features of the new power of attorney statute.

1. A power of attorney executed after September 30, 2011 goes into effect immediately upon signing. Accordingly, the new power of attorney statute eliminates "Springing Powers of Attorney". A Springing Power of Attorney is a power of attorney, which would go into effect at a later date, after the power of attorney was signed.

2. A "general grant of authority" can no longer be effectively used under the new law. Additionally, certain authorities granted in the power of attorney document must be specifically delineated, and separately signed or initialed by the principal.

Examples of the types of powers that must be initiated or signed by the principal are as follows:

- The creation of a living trust.
- Amendment, modification, revocation or termination of a

trust created by or on behalf of the principal.

- Make a gift.
- Create or change a right of survivorship.
- The creation or changing of a beneficiary designation.
- The waiver of the principal's right to be beneficiary of a joint and survivor annuity, including a survivor benefit under a retirement plan.
- Disclaiming property or a power of appointment.

Under the new power of attorney statute, the agent must meet certain criteria. The agent must be a natural person who is at least 18 years of age, or is a financial institution that has trust powers, has a place of business in Florida, and is authorized to conduct trust business in Florida.

Under the new statute, certain types of powers are prohibited by the agent. The following powers are prohibited:

- The Agent cannot perform duties under a contract that requires personal services of the principal.
- The Agent cannot make an affidavit as to the personal knowledge of the Principal.
- The Agent cannot vote in a public election on behalf of the principal.
- The Agent cannot execute or revoke any Will or codicil for the principal.
- The Agent cannot exercise any powers or authority granted to the principal as trustee or as court-appointed fiduciary.

Other details regarding the Agent under the new power of attorney statute are as follows:

- Co-Agents may be appointed, and either agent can act

independently, unless stated otherwise in the power of attorney document.

- Successor Agents can be appointed in the power of attorney document.
- Any Agent is entitled to be reimbursed for expenses.
- Only a "Qualified Agent" can be paid compensation. Qualified Agents are the following individuals: a spouse or heir of the principal, a financial institution with trust powers and a place of business in Florida, an attorney or a certified public accountant licensed in Florida, or a natural person who is a Florida resident and who had never been an agent for more than three principals at the same time.

There are also significant new rules regarding the acceptance or rejection of the power of attorney document by third parties:

- The third party must accept or reject the power of attorney within a reasonable period of time.
- For financial institutions, there is a presumption that four days is a reasonable period of time.
- For other third parties, the reasonableness of the acceptance or rejection of the power of attorney will depend on the facts and circumstances, and the terms stated in the power of attorney document.
- If the power of attorney is rejected, the reasons for the rejection must be stated in writing.
- A third party is not required to accept the power of attorney under the following circumstances:
  1. The third party is not obligated to engage in the transaction with the principal.
  2. The third party is aware that the Agent's authority has been suspended or terminated.

3. If the third party has made a timely request for an affidavit or English translation, or an opinion of counsel.

4. The third party has good faith belief that the power of attorney is not valid, or the Agent does not have authority.

5. The third party has knowledge of a report to Adult Protective Services supporting a good faith belief that the principal may be subject to financial or physical abuse by the Agent or someone acting with the Agent.

Other important features of the new power of attorney statute are as follows:

- If the third party improperly rejects the power of attorney, the third party is liable for damages, including attorneys fees and costs; and the third party is also subject to a court order which would impose acceptance of the power of attorney or the third party.

- If the third party accepts the power of attorney in good faith, the third party will be held harmless for loss suffered by the principal.

- The filing of a petition for divorce or annulment terminates the spouse's authority to act as the agent under the power of attorney.

- A military power of attorney will continue to be recognized as valid under Florida law, if the military power of attorney is executed in accordance 10 U.S.C. § 1044b.

With respect to Medicaid planning, two of the most significant issues to be addressed under the new power of attorney statute are the following: the use of a power of attorney to execute a Qualified Income Trusts, and the use of a power of attorney to execute personal service contracts. Since a general grant of authority is no longer authorized under the new power of attorney statute, the Florida Department of

Children and Families will require the separate initialing or signature of specified provisions in the power of attorney document to establish a qualified income trust if the power of attorney document was executed on or after October 1, 2011.

Avoiding Probate and Medicaid Benefit Recovery

Probate is a court-ordered proceeding during which the assets of a deceased individual are accounted for, and then distributed to the beneficiaries named in the deceased individual's Will.[35]

The typical probate situation happens when individuals die while they own assets in their name, with no co-owner or beneficiary listed on the assets. For example, if a person dies while they own an individual checking account, and there are no co-owners or payable-on-death beneficiaries on that checking account, the only way to transfer title is through the probate process. No one has legal authority to do anything with the account without court approval.

If the account holder had issued a power of attorney to an attorney-in-fact (the person who was appointed to act on behalf of the principle of the power of attorney) when the principle was alive, the authority of the power of attorney ends with death. A court order, issued by the probate court, would be required to transfer title out of the deceased individual's name and into the names of the beneficiaries.

The significance of probate, as it relates to Florida Medicaid, is that the probate process is the primary way that Medicaid benefits can potentially be paid back to the State of Florida.[36] Florida requires that notice be given to creditors, and the law requires probate estates, of any deceased individual over the age of 55, to serve notice to the Agency for Health Care Administration. This process ensures that the Agency for Health Care Administration will have notice of the probate estate of elderly Medicaid beneficiaries. It will enable the state to recover against any nonexempt assets in the deceased individual's estate.

One asset against which the state cannot usually recover is a Florida homestead.[37] The Florida state constitution provides protection of a homestead against most creditors; however, for it to remain exempt from creditors during the probate process, the homestead property must be inherited by the heirs of the deceased individual.

Example 1: Mildred was an 86-year-old Florida resident who received ICP Medicaid benefits at a skilled nursing facility for the last three years of her life.

When she died, she owned a checking account worth $800. She also had a term life insurance policy with no cash value, but it had a $20,000 death benefit.

Mildred failed to list any beneficiaries on the life insurance policy. Mildred's only child, Jessica, called the life insurance company when Mildred died. Jessica was told by the insurance company that she would need "Letters of Administration," issued by a Florida probate court, for anyone to have access to the life insurance policy.

Jessica hired an attorney to open a probate. When the probate was opened, the Agency for Health Care Administration was notified of Mildred's probate proceeding, in accordance with Florida statutes.

The Medicaid lien for Mildred's three years of care ended up exceeding $120,000. Because the Medicaid lien exceeded the value of the assets of the estate, there was nothing left for Jessica to inherit after AHCA was paid its claim.

Example 2: Assume the same facts as in Example 1, except in this example, the only asset of Mildred's estate is the Florida homestead property.

When the Florida home went through probate, the Agency for Health Care Administration was notified. AHCA filed a claim against the estate; however, in this example, the homestead is a protected asset under the Florida constitution, and Jessica is Mildred's natural heir.

Jessica received the homestead property, and AHCA was not able to recover against the homestead property, because the property was exempt, and was inherited by Mildred's natural heir, Jessica.

Income Allocation for the Community Spouse (Income Diversion)

When one spouse needs long-term care in a nursing home and one spouse is able to remain at home, the matter of income allocation (also called income diversion) becomes an issue. In some situations, however, the spouse who earns the bulk of the income for the household is the nursing home resident. If the community spouse's income is low enough, Florida law allows for the community spouse to receive some or all of the institutionalized spouse's income. There are three basic income allocation definitions:

The minimum monthly maintenance income allowance. This is the minimum dollar amount the community spouse will receive, between the community spouse's income and the institutionalized spouse's income. The minimum monthly maintenance income allowance for 2012 is $1,839.

Example: Lucien is a 92-year-old resident of Manatee County, Florida, who is married to 89-year-old Nicole.

Lucien needs long-term care at a nursing home, but Nicole is still able to live in the community by herself.

Lucien receives $1,800 in Social Security, and Nicole receives $200 in Social Security. They have only $50,000 in countable assets between the two of them, and Nicole lives in their $200,000 Bradenton, Florida home, which is fully paid for.

Nicole has monthly shelter expenses which are less than the $552 per month excess shelter standard. Nicole will be entitled to the minimum monthly needs allowance, which means she will keep her $200 per month in Social Security and will also receive $1,639 of Lucien's monthly income (for a total of $1,839 income for Nicole).

Lucien's patient responsibility will be: $126 ($1,800 - $1,639 - $35 = $126).

The maximum monthly maintenance income allowance. This number is the total maximum dollar amount the community spouse can receive each month if the community spouse is receiving income allocation from the institutionalized spouse. The maximum monthly maintenance income allowance in 2012 is $2,841.

The excess shelter standard. The excess shelter standard are the dollar amount of shelter expenses that the community spouse needs to exceed to receive more than the minimum monthly maintenance needs allowance of $1,839. If the community spouse has shelter expenses that exceed the excess shelter standard, the community spouse is entitled to receive more than the minimum monthly maintenance allowance. The excess shelter standard for 2012 is $552.

Example: Alfred and Beatrice are married residents of Liberty County, Florida, and both are over the age of 65.

Alfred needs long-term nursing home care, and his income is $2,200 per month. Beatrice's monthly income is $400 per month, and she lives in an apartment which rents for $2,600 per month.

Assuming all other eligibility requirements are met, Beatrice will be able to keep all of Alfred's income of $2,200 per month because her shelter expenses (monthly rent) are so high. Between her income of $400 per month, and his income of $2,200 per month (which is less than the maximum maintenance income allowance of $2,841), Beatrice would be entitled to keep all income sources, and the cost of the nursing home would be zero.

Medicare

Medicare is a government health insurance program that is separate and distinct from Medicaid. Although Medicare is generally designed for people who are 65 or older, under certain circumstances individuals under the age of 65 may also be eligible. For example, if a person under the age of 65 is receiving Social Security Disability Income, that person may also be eligible for Medicare benefits.

The primary Medicare programs encountered when applying for Medicaid are the following:

1. Medicare Part A
2. Medicare Part B
3. Medicare Part D

Medicare Part A. Individuals who have paid into Social Security or Railroad Retirement during their careers become automatically eligible for Medicare Part A upon reaching the age of 65. There is generally no charge for Part A. It pays for a portion of hospitalization expenses, and for short periods of time and under certain conditions, for rehabilitation stays in skilled nursing facilities. Medicare Part A does not cover long-term stays at nursing facilities.

If certain criteria are met, Medicare Part A may cover the cost of nursing rehabilitation stays from 1–20 days. Medicare Part A may, if certain medical criteria are met, provide a partial payment to the skilled nursing facility for between days 21 and 100.

Medicare Part B. A portion of outpatient expenses is paid by Medicare Part B for physician's office visits. To receive Medicare Part B benefits, an amount is deducted each month from a person's Social Security check. For the year 2012, the Medicare Part B program premium is $99.90 per month (for most people). However, other beneficiaries will be subject to paying a $115.40 Medicare Part B program premium due to factors such as their income, or because they are new enrollees, or they do not have their Part B premiums withheld from Social Security benefits payments. Higher income earners can have an even higher Medicare Part B premium, above $115.40 per month.

Medicare Part D. Also known as "the prescription drug program," Medicare Part D is frequently an issue in Medicaid planning. Medicare Part D is a relatively new program, which began in January 2006, to help Medicare beneficiaries pay for their prescription drugs.

The Medicare Part D program requires individuals to choose one of hundreds of Medicare Part D prescription drug programs, which are offered by private health insurance companies. There is a premium for Medicare Part D coverage, and the premium will be dependent on the drug plan selected and the insurance company that the individual has selected. As with the Medicare Part B plan, the Medicare Part D premium is deducted directly from the individual's Social Security check each month.

It's not always mandatory to sign up for Medicare Part D. If a person has health insurance that covers the cost of prescription drugs (referred to as "creditable coverage"), they may have no need for Medicare Part D. However, if a person has no "creditable" health insurance coverage and they receive Medicaid benefits in Florida, the individual must select a Medicare Part D prescription drug program, or the State of Florida will select a Medicare Part D plan for them.

Individual Retirement Accounts (IRAs) — Assets or Income Sources?

Individual retirement accounts (IRAs) have characteristics of both assets and income sources. On one hand, IRAs often have significant value. On the other hand, if withdrawals are made from IRA's, they usually constitute taxable income in the year of the withdrawal.[38] The *Policy Manual* states that if "an individual is eligible to receive regular periodic payments, then the IRA is not considered a countable asset."[39]

The *Policy Manual* also states that, for the IRA to be considered a non-countable asset, the Medicaid applicant must actually take distributions for which he or she is eligible.

Example: Walter is a 78-year-old man confined to a nursing home in Marion County, Florida.

Walter has already spent most of his life savings on the nursing home. He has $1,500 left in his checking account, he receives $600 per month in gross Social Security, and he has a $40,000 IRA that pays him $300 per month.

The $300 per month exceeds all income generated by the assets that comprise the IRA, and the $300 per month paid to Walter each month represents the required minimum distribution (RMD). The IRA custodian has calculated the RMD, so the IRA distribution would comply with US Treasury Department rules.

In this situation, Walter's IRA will be treated as a non-countable asset, because the monthly payment Walter receives from the IRA complies with *The Policy Manual* rule; Walter actually takes the IRA distributions of $300 per month for which he is eligible.[40]

Long-Term Care Insurance

Long-term care insurance is a type of private insurance that can be purchased by individuals who medically qualify for it. Long-term care insurance can provide coverage for nursing homes, assisted living facilities, and for in-home coverage. The cost is dependent on a number of criteria:

- the age and health of person to be covered
- the amount and length of time a person would be covered under the policy
- the rating of the insurance company
- exclusions and inclusions of the policy
- whether or not the policy will be adjusted for inflation

Unfortunately, it is not uncommon for individuals who have long-term care insurance to also have to apply for Medicaid benefits – after they are admitted to a skilled nursing facility. Long-term care insurance policies are often purchased many years prior to their use, and the policy has a stated daily payment that is often not adjusted for inflation. With the average daily cost of skilled nursing care often exceeding $170 per day in Florida, many long-term care insurance policies do not provide sufficient payments to cover the cost of long-term care in a nursing home.

This observation is intended neither to discourage readers from purchasing long-term care insurance nor to encourage individuals to drop their current long-term care insurance. It is, however, a reminder to the reader to understand the importance of knowing exactly what a policy will cover, how much the policy will pay, what the policy exclusions are, and whether or not the policy will be adjusted for inflation.

There are generally two types of long-term care insurance policies: an indemnity policy and a reimbursement policy:

1. An *indemnity* policy is a policy that will pay a fixed, per-day dollar amount while the person is eligible to receive the benefits. For example, the indemnity policy may pay $70 per day, while the person is in the nursing home or assisted living facility.

2. A *reimbursement* policy repays to the covered individual some of the cost of the facility – up to a certain dollar amount.

If a covered person receives an indemnity payment from a policy, the payment will be treated as income (for purposes of the Florida income cap). This can make it necessary to have a Qualified Income Trust, if the person has to apply for Medicaid benefits. However, if the long-term care insurance policy makes reimbursement payments, the payments will generally not be treated as income (for purposes of the Florida income cap).

Example: Sylvia is an 86-year-old resident of Gainesville, Florida who needs long-term care in a skilled nursing facility.

Sylvia's only asset is $1,500 in her checking account. She receives $800 per month in gross Social Security, and she has a long-term care insurance policy that makes an indemnity payment of $50 per day.

The nursing home she resides in costs $200 per day, so with her Social Security and her $50 per day, she falls well short of being able to pay for the facility privately.

Because the indemnity payment of $50 per day is going to be treated as income according to the *Policy Manual*, she will now exceed the $2,094 income cap for 2012: $800 Social Security + ($50 indemnity x 30 days) = $2,300 in gross income per month.

Sylvia, her attorney-in-fact, or her guardian will need to establish, and properly fund every month, a Qualified Income Trust so that Sylvia can receive Medicaid benefits.

Most long-term care insurance policies make indemnity payments, rather than reimbursement payments. If a person who is covered by a long-term care policy needs to apply for Medicaid, an indemnity payment will usually cause the person to exceed the income cap and make it necessary for the individual to have a Qualified Income Trust.

Life Estate Deeds and Enhanced Life Estate Deeds (Lady Bird Deeds)

Many individuals seek ways to avoid the probate process. One way to avoid probate with real property is with the use of a life estate deed.[41]

If a Medicaid applicant grants a remainder interest to anyone using a "life estate" deed, it often means a transfer, for less than fair market value, of the remainder interest. The remainder interest of a life estate deed is a future interest in real property that the remainder beneficiaries possess. When the life estate holder dies, the remainder beneficiaries of the deed become the fully vested owners of the property.

The transfer of the remainder interest can create a disqualification period for Medicaid, depending on the date and the value of the property interest transferred.

> **Example:** Isabella is an 87-year-old resident of Tarpon Springs, Florida.
>
> Isabella recently suffered a stroke, and now needs long-term care in a skilled nursing facility.
>
> Six months ago, Isabella added her only daughter, Libertad, to the deed as a "remainder beneficiary," by executing a life estate deed. At the time of the transfer, the fair market value of the property was $300,000. According to the *Policy Manual*, the value of the life interest retained by Isabella was $96,786 ($300,000 x .67738).
>
> The transfer of the remainder interest transferred to Libertad will create a significant disqualification period of Medicaid for Isabella.

A way to avoid the problem created in the previous example is with the use of an "enhanced life estate" deed or a "Lady Bird" deed. If drafted properly, an enhanced life estate deed will avoid probate and *not* create a disqualification for Medicaid.

CHAPTER 8

Veterans Benefits

Veterans Benefits may be available to elderly veterans, or their surviving spouses, under certain circumstances. If the Medicaid applicant is a veteran (or the surviving spouse of a deceased veteran), the Florida Department of Children and Families caseworker will often require that an application for Veterans Benefits be filed with the Department of Veterans Affairs (VA) before the Medicaid application is approved. Any benefit received by the veteran (or the surviving spouse) will transfer some of the cost burden paid out by the Medicaid program to the Veterans Administration.

Because the approval of Veterans Benefits typically takes several months, the DCF caseworker will not require proof of an actual *approval* of Veterans Benefits; the caseworker will only require proof that the person has actually *applied* for the Veterans Benefits.

Under some circumstances, Veterans Benefits can be quite significant. There are even certain situations where the Department of Veterans Affairs may pay for the entire cost of nursing home care, which would eliminate the need to apply for Medicaid benefits. However, these circumstances are rather rare.

There are two general categories of Veterans Benefits: **service connected benefits** (compensation) and **non-service connected benefits** (pension). There are also other important concepts related to eligibility for Veterans Benefits.

One requirement is that of having performed active service in the US military, which, incidentally, does include a broader scope than just the US Army, Navy, Air Force, Marines and Coast Guard. Prior membership in the Merchant Marines, the Woman's Army Auxiliary Corps, or the National Oceanic and Atmosphere Administration (NOAA), as well as several other organizations, may lead to eligibility for Veterans Benefits. The US Department of Veterans Affairs can be contacted for a complete list of all organizations that may lead to eligibility for Veterans Benefits by calling 1-800-827-1000, or visiting their website at http://www.va.gov/.

As a general rule, other requirements are that the active service must have occurred during a period of wartime (at least one day), the veteran must have actively served a minimum of 90 days, and the discharge from service must be for other than a "dishonorable" reason. However, if the discharge is not "honorable," the reason for the discharge should be investigated further to make sure there will be no effect on eligibility for VA benefits. Additionally, there are different service requirements for veterans who enlisted after September 7, 1980.

Service Connected Disability Benefits (Compensation)

If a veteran meets the criteria for active service and becomes disabled as the result of an injury during active service (or a disability that is aggravated as the result of active service), the veteran will be eligible for Service Connected Disability Benefits.

VA can pay monthly compensation if the veteran is at least 10% disabled as a result of military service.

Who Qualifies for Service Connected Benefits?

Service Requirements:

To qualify for service connected benefits, the veteran will have to have sustained injuries or diseases as a result of their military service while on active duty. In addition, if an injury or a disease was made worse by the rigors of active duty, then the veteran will be able to collect benefits.

Those who have not sustained injuries as a result of active duty or had worsening injuries as a result of active duty do not qualify for the service connected benefits. Others who do not qualify for these benefits include those who injured themselves through willful misconduct or from the abuse of drugs and/or alcohol.

Disability Requirements:

To receive benefits from the Veteran's Administration for disabilities, a veteran must undergo medical testing. This will allow the veteran's disability to be rated.

More than 2.9 million veterans have applied for this veteran's benefit, more than any other benefit provided by the Veteran's Administration. There are three main requirements that will need to be met in order for a veteran to qualify for disability compensation:

1. The veteran needs to show evidence of a current medical condition or disability.

2. There needs to be a statement that the injury or illness occurred while on active duty.

3. A clear connection needs to be made between the injury or condition and the occurrence during active duty.

Determining the connection between the event and the injury can be problematic, leading to delays in compensation, especially when the injury occurred a long time ago. However, the case can be appealed to higher authorities if the veteran is unable to get his or her benefits approved.

Gathering as much evidence as possible will help to increase the odds that the claim is accepted and benefits are paid.

Working with the military as well as a physician to assemble these records will help the veteran have all of the necessary information for their benefits application process.

If a condition is not immediately obvious, then the veteran will need to submit a statement of their disability to the SSA as well as to the Veteran's Administration by a physician or a certified psychiatrist or psychologist.

How Does the VA Evaluate Levels of Disability?

Once the veteran is determined to be eligible for disability compensation, the next step is for the VA to evaluate the extent of the disability. A rating system — called the Schedule for Rating Disabilities — is used to categorize a veteran's degree of disability resulting from service-connected injuries.

The disability rating determines the benefit payments to be awarded to the veteran for their specific condition.

The disability levels range from a low of 10% disability up to a maximum of 100% disability, with 10% interval classifications between. If the disability worsens over time, it is possible for the veteran to increase his or her level of disability classification, creating a higher level of benefit payment.

As many as 1.2 million veterans are given a rating of zero (0). This usually means the VA has determined that a veteran has a condition that can be classified as service connected; however, it is not severe enough to qualify for monetary compensation based on the medical criteria specified in the rating schedule.

Other veterans may have more than one disability. In these cases, the disability rating is figured by the VA rating schedule using a formula for a combined evaluation of medical criteria and disability ratings. However, two individual disability ratings are not simply added together to produce a larger, final percentage. In fact, often one of the two numbers is chosen when the rating description matches the entire disability's situation more reasonably. For example, a veteran has trouble with his or her legs, which makes it difficult to walk, but the veteran also has a stiff shoulder. The leg might be given a higher disability rating as the leg issue is more representative of how the disabilities affect the veteran.

Each disability reviewer is different too, so that will play a role in how the veteran's rating is measured. Since no rating can be completely objective, the veteran may need to have their case reviewed several times before they feel their rating is satisfactory

Total Disability

When a veteran is not able to be gainfully employed again, they are considered to be totally disabled. The conditions which can be a part of total disability include:

- Loss of use of one or both hands
- Loss of use of one or both feet
- Lost of sight in both eyes
- Person is bedridden
- Person is helpless to care for themselves

More Than One Rating is Possible

Disabilities that occur as a result of the primary disability will also need to have their own ratings. For example, if someone has a foot problem as a result of active duty, that person might also develop arthritis as a result, but this would get its own rating.

Those who start at a 0% may find their disability rating goes up as the years pass, as their injuries become more problematic and intrusive. Having injuries reassessed will help a veteran secure the benefits owed to them because of injuries suffered as a result of active duty.

Service Connected Benefits Are Not Needs Based

What many do not realize is that the service connected benefits program for veterans is not based on needs. This means the income level of the veteran as well as the resources the veteran has access to will not be counted or considered to determine the benefits to be paid.

Some of the benefits will arrive as money distributed at regular intervals, with the amounts changing each year, as determined by the Veteran's Administration.

Again, one's income is not included in the distribution of the funds. Only the severity of the disability can help to change the amount of money a veteran might receive from the Veteran's Administration.

What Are Presumptive Conditions?

When a veteran has been in certain situations, they automatically qualify for disability payments from the VA. These conditions include:

- Veterans exposed to radiation while on active duty.
- Veterans exposed to Agent Orange or other herbicides.
- Prisoners of war (POWs).
- Gulf War veterans who have chronic disabilities as a result of their service.

When a veteran has been in any of these situations, they will receive regular payments to help compensate them for injuries which may have occurred — or which have yet to occur — from the dangerous situations and war times.

While these conditions may be simple to prove, documentation will still be necessary to receive the benefits.

What Is Combat-Related Special Compensation?

Those veterans who were injured during times of combat are eligible for combat-related special compensation (CRSC). This is a payment which is distributed in addition to the veteran's retirement pay and their VA disability compensation.

However, there are certain criteria a veteran has to meet to receive these benefits:

- The veteran must also be receiving military retired pay.
- The veteran must be medically retired with 20 years of credible service.
- The VA injury must be 10% or higher.

These special compensation benefits are applied for alongside the other benefits that come along with service connected disabilities.

What Compensation Looks Like
With and Without Dependents

The figures for the service connected disability benefits also will fluctuate based on the number of dependents the veteran might have. The more dependents who are present, the higher the benefits, in addition to having a higher benefit when the disability rating is higher.

Currently, the VA compensation rates are for those veterans with a disability rating of over 10%, effective in December of 2011 are:

With or Without Dependents (monthly benefits)

Disability rating of 10% = $127
Disability rating of 20% = $251

For Those Without Dependents
30 to 60% Disability Rating

continued

Without Dependents (monthly benefits), Veteran Alone

Disability rating of 30% = $389
Disability rating of 40% = $560
Disability rating of 50% = $797
Disability rating of 60% = $1009

Without Dependents (monthly benefits), Veteran with Spouse

Disability rating of 30% = $435
Disability rating of 40% = $622
Disability rating of 50% = $874
Disability rating of 60% = $1102

Without Dependents (monthly benefits), Veteran, Spouse, and One Parent

Disability rating of 30% = $472
Disability rating of 40% = $671
Disability rating of 50% = $936
Disability rating of 60% = $1176

Without Dependents (monthly benefits), Veteran, Spouse, and Two Parents

Disability rating of 30% = $509
Disability rating of 40% = $720
Disability rating of 50% = $998
Disability rating of 60% = $1250

Without Dependents (monthly benefits), Veteran and One Parent

Disability rating of 30% = $426
Disability rating of 40% = $609
Disability rating of 50% = $859
Disability rating of 60% = $1083

Without Dependents (monthly benefits), Veteran with Two Parents

Disability rating of 30% = $463
Disability rating of 40% = $658
Disability rating of 50% = $921
Disability rating of 60% = $1157

Without Dependents, Additional Compensation
for Spouse Who Needs Assistance

Disability rating of 30% = $42
Disability rating of 40% = $56
Disability rating of 50% = $71
Disability rating of 60% = $84

70 to 100% Disability Rating

Without Dependents (monthly benefits), Veteran Alone

Disability rating of 70% = $1272
Disability rating of 80% = $1478
Disability rating of 90% = $1661
Disability rating of 100% = $2769

Without Dependents (monthly benefits), Veteran and Spouse

Disability rating of 70% = $1380
Disability rating of 80% = $1602
Disability rating of 90% = $1800
Disability rating of 100% = $2924

Without Dependents (monthly benefits), Veteran, Spouse, and One Parent

Disability rating of 70% = $1466
Disability rating of 80% = $1701
Disability rating of 90% = $1911
Disability rating of 100% = $3048

Without Dependents (monthly benefits),
Veteran, Spouse and Two Parents

Disability rating of 70% = $1552
Disability rating of 80% = $1800
Disability rating of 90% = $2022
Disability rating of 100% = $3172

Without Dependents (monthly benefits), Veteran and One Parent

Disability rating of 70% = $1358
Disability rating of 80% = $1577
Disability rating of 90% = $1772
Disability rating of 100% = $2893

Without Dependents (monthly benefits), Veteran and Two Parents

Disability rating of 70% = $1444
Disability rating of 80% = $1676
Disability rating of 90% = $1883
Disability rating of 100% = $3017

Additional Compensation for Spouse Who Needs Assistance

Disability rating of 70% = $99
Disability rating of 80% = $112
Disability rating of 90% = $127
Disability rating of 100% = $141

For Those With Dependents
30 to 60% Disability Rating

With Dependents, (monthly benefits), Veteran, Spouse, and Child

Disability rating of 30% = $469
Disability rating of 40% = $667
Disability rating of 50% = $931
Disability rating of 60% = $1169

With Dependents, (monthly benefits), Veteran with Child Only

Disability rating of 30% = $420
Disability rating of 40% = $601
Disability rating of 50% = $849
Disability rating of 60% = $1071

With Dependents, (monthly benefits),
Veteran, Spouse, One Parent and Child

Disability rating of 30% = $506
Disability rating of 40% = $716
Disability rating of 50% = $993
Disability rating of 60% = $1243

With Dependents, (monthly benefits),
Veteran, Spouse, Two Parents and Child

Disability rating of 30% = $543
Disability rating of 40% = $765
Disability rating of 50% = $1055
Disability rating of 60% = $1317

With Dependents, (monthly benefits), Veteran with One Parent and Child

    Disability rating of 30% = $457
    Disability rating of 40% = $650
    Disability rating of 50% = $911
    Disability rating of 60% = $1145

With Dependents, (monthly benefits), Veteran with Two Parents and Child

    Disability rating of 30% = $494
    Disability rating of 40% = $699
    Disability rating of 50% = $973
    Disability rating of 60% = $1219

Add for Each Additional Child Under 18

    Disability rating of 30% = $23
    Disability rating of 40% = $30
    Disability rating of 50% = $38
    Disability rating of 60% = $46

Add for Each Additional Child Over 18 Who is Attending School

    Disability rating of 30% = $74
    Disability rating of 40% = $99
    Disability rating of 50% = $124
    Disability rating of 60% = $148

Additional Compensation for Spouse Who Needs Assistance

    Disability rating of 30% = $42
    Disability rating of 40% = $56
    Disability rating of 50% = $71

Disability rating of 60% = $84

70 to 100% Disability Rating

With Dependents, (monthly benefits), Veteran, Spouse and Child

Disability rating of 70% = $1459
Disability rating of 80% = $1692
Disability rating of 90% = $1902
Disability rating of 100% = $3037

With Dependents, (monthly benefits), Veteran and Child Only

Disability rating of 70% = $1344
Disability rating of 80% = $1561
Disability rating of 90% = $1754
Disability rating of 100% = $2873

With Dependents, (monthly benefits),
Veteran, Spouse, One Parent and Child

Disability rating of 70% = $1545
Disability rating of 80% = $1791
Disability rating of 90% = $2013
Disability rating of 100% = $3161

With Dependents, (monthly benefits),
Veteran, Spouse, Two Parents and Child

Disability rating of 70% = $1631
Disability rating of 80% = $1890
Disability rating of 90% = $2124
Disability rating of 100% = $3285

With Dependents, (monthly benefits),
Veteran with One Parent and Child

Disability rating of 70% = $1430
Disability rating of 80% = $1660
Disability rating of 90% = $1865
Disability rating of 100% = $2997

With Dependents, (monthly benefits),
Veteran with Two Parents and Child

Disability rating of 70% = $1516
Disability rating of 80% = $1759
Disability rating of 90% = $1976
Disability rating of 100% = $3121

Add for Each Additional Child Under 18

Disability rating of 70% = $53
Disability rating of 80% = $61
Disability rating of 90% = $69
Disability rating of 100% = $77

Add for Each Additional Child Over 18 Who is Attending School

Disability rating of 70% = $173
Disability rating of 80% = $198
Disability rating of 90% = $223
Disability rating of 100% = $248

Additional Compensation for Spouse Who Needs Assistance

Disability rating of 70% = $99
Disability rating of 80% = $112
Disability rating of 90% = $127
Disability rating of 100% = $141

Other Service Connected Benefits

Many veterans will also automatically qualify if they have certain conditions and disability ratings. Veterans are able to receive more than just monthly payments. Knowing what is available for their personal use will allow veterans to save money on health care.

While this list is not exhaustive, it provides a summary of some of the service connected benefits available.

Long-Term Care

- Nursing home care is covered if the veteran is seeking nursing home care for a service related injury, condition, or diseases.

- Veterans with a disability rating of 60%+ and who cannot work qualify for unlimited nursing home care.

- Veterans with a disability rating of 70%+ qualify for unlimited nursing home care.

Co-payments

- Veterans who are seeking care for a service connected disability do not have to pay a co-payment on medical visits which pertain to that condition.

Prescriptions

- Veterans with disability ratings of more than 50% do not have to pay for prescriptions.

- Veterans who use a medication for a service connected disability do not have to pay for medication.

Life Insurance

Veterans who can prove they have a service connected disability will also be able to retain life insurance policies as a part of their benefits as a veteran and they will be able to apply for additional disabled veteran's insurance, which has low rates.

Disabled Transition Assistance Program (DTAP)

This program allows veterans to learn more about whether they qualify for assistance through the VA's Vocational Rehabilitation and Employment program. This program allows a veteran to fill out an application for vocational rehabilitation benefits.

At these presentations, veterans will be able to discuss DTAP and decide whether this program applies to their lives. Sessions can even be coordinated to accommodate those veterans who might be in the hospital, an assisted living facility, or are simply unable to go to one of the sessions.

Veterans might even want to bring their medical records to help them review their case with trained professionals.

Service Connected Benefits by Disability Rating

There are a number of benefits which are possible when a service connected disability has been recognized. Learning the details of what you might be able to take advantage of will allow you to not only save money, but also have peace of mind for yourself and for your family.

0% and Higher

- Home Loan Guaranty Certificate of Eligibility
- $10,000 Life Insurance Policy — Veterans must file within the

two-year span of filing for their service connected disability.

- Outpatient treatment for conditions related to service injuries.
- Travel allowance to VA facilities for scheduled appointments for service connected conditions. (Based on income level or 25+ miles distance traveled from home.)
- Medical treatment for any condition, if enrolled in VA health-care program.
- VA doctor prescribed prosthetic devices including tanks of oxygen, wheelchairs, nebulizers, canes, crutches, hospital beds, motorized scooters, and other related equipment, depending on the circumstance.
- Medical treatment with VA issued and authorized fee basis card in non-VA facilities for service connected conditions.
- Civil Service Preference — Ten (10) points added to a Civil Service test score if 70 or higher score obtained by the veteran.
- Yearly clothing allowance of $741 for veterans with a service connected condition requiring the use of a VA prescribed prosthetic appliance or who use VA prescribed medications for a skin condition which wears or soils articles of clothing.
- Temporary 100% rating, when hospitalized for a service connected disability. This rating requires at least one month of immobilization by cast and/or recuperation.
- Dental treatment or follow-up treatment for a service connected condition. Former POWs with 90+ consecutive days of confinement also receive this treatment.
- Home Improvement and Structural Alteration Grant Program: Service connected veterans can receive up to a $4,100 grant while non-service connected veterans may receive a grant up to $1,200 for improving their homes to provide accessibility for injuries and disabilities.

10% and Higher, all of the above plus:

- Vocational rehabilitation which includes full medical and dental care, an allowance (as well as disability payments), payment for all school-related supplies which are required by the program, and tuition payments to the school.
- Home loan guaranty loans will not require funding fee.

30% and Higher, all of the above plus:

- Additional monetary compensation for dependents.
- Job appointment without an interview to civil service position.
- Employment affirmative action.
- Additional allowance for a spouse in long-term care facility.

40% and Higher, all of the above plus:

- One time automobile grant of up to $18,900.
- Payment for adaptive devices for the automobile related to disability.

50% or Higher, all of the above plus:

- $0 co-payment for treatment of non-service connected care or prescription drugs.
- Medical treatment with fee basis card in non-VA facilities for any condition.

60–90% or Higher, all of the above plus:

- Increased compensation for veteran, payable at the 100% rate if unable to work due to service connected disability.

100% or Complete Loss of Employability, all of the above plus:

- Unlimited dental treatment.

- Educational funding for dependents – some restrictions apply.

- CHAMPVA benefits – Health and medical program for survivors and dependents.

- Grants up to 50% of a home's cost (no more than $63,780) for building, purchasing, or remodeling homes to be supportive of disabilities. These grants can also help to pay toward a balance on an existing home mortgage.

- Grants up to $12,756 to assist in adapting a veteran's home or to acquire a new or previously owned residence which is already adapted for the disability.

- Veteran's mortgage life insurance – Decreasing term mortgage insurance up to $90,000 for veterans who have received a Specially Adaptive Housing grant and who already have an existing mortgage.

- Waiver of cost of life insurance.

- Additional $10,000 of life insurance.

- Commissary privileges for veteran and dependents of disabled veteran.

- Exchange privileges for veterans and dependents of disabled veteran

- Emergency treatment in non-VA facilities if VA facilities are unavailable.

- Yearly eye exams and prescribed eyewear.

- Special compensation, based on disability ratings and other special situations.

How to Secure Service Connected Disability Benefits

To receive the service connected disability payments, you will need to do some legwork. Note that persistence can be a valuable trait to have when you are continuing this process.

1. Find the nearest veteran's service organization

    Here, you will begin the process of filling out forms and finding out what information will be needed by the Veteran's Administration. In some cases, you may simply need to call the office or look at a website, but often going to an office in person can help expedite the process. However, this may also not be possible due to the disability's limitations.

    These organizations will also have people on staff who are able to navigate the process for you and work for your best interests. The services are free and the paperwork can be sent directly to your physician or therapist for further documentation.

    The form you will need to fill out and submit along with documentation is VA form 21-526.

2. Gather all medication and psychological documentation

    The more records you can have to support your case, the more smoothly the application process can be. It will be ideal for you to collect as many medical records as you can, then make copies of these records to ensure you have backup records as needed.

    You will need to have the following documents, in addition to the documentation of the disability:

    - List of disabilities you are claiming.
    - Copy of your DD214.
    - Marriage license.
    - Birth certificates of dependents.

3. Be patient, but follow up.

It never hurts to find someone in the Veteran's Administration to call to follow up on your application. This way, you can quickly find out whether your application was approved or denied. Give the VA some time to review your documentation (especially when there is a lot), but follow up regularly if you feel that the process is slower than it should be.

4. If you should be denied:

If your disability claim is denied or your disability rating isn't as high as you might expect it to be, it's a good idea to appeal the decision as quickly as possible. You need to make sure you are reading all of the paperwork which comes from the VA to your home to ensure you are getting the necessary documentation to the VA. In some cases, you may have been asked to submit more files or to resubmit different copies of a medical record, so reading all of your VA paperwork completely may help you to avoid having to appeal their decision.

In some cases, you can work with the veteran's service organization to help see what else you can do to increase the odds of your application being approved. Benefits are applied retroactively, so it is encouraged that you file your appeal as soon as you can.

Talk with your doctor and show them the denial letter you received. They can then write to the VA themselves to refute any arguments which may have been presented. Together, you can work to ensure that you receive the disability benefits you deserve.

That said, the appeal process can take time.

5. If you are approved:

If you get the disability rating that you qualify for, then you will begin to receive the payments on a monthly basis, while also receiving the ability to get VA health care for your disability at no charge to you.

Note too that you can apply to have your disability rating increased or decreased as necessary. Talking with your medical care professional will help you begin this process again if you need to make changes in the way the military supports your health and your family needs.

In this way, you can be certain your commitment to the military doesn't affect the quality of your life once you are honorably discharged.

Non-Service Connected Veterans Benefits (VA Improved Pension or Pension)

When dealing with Medicaid applications, a Veterans Benefit referred to as "Aid and Attendance" is the program most commonly encountered. If the veteran meets the basic eligibility criteria described below, and the veteran (or spouse) needs assistance from another person with the activities of daily living, then the veteran will qualify for the Aid and Attendance benefit. Aid and Attendance is particularly important in the assisted living setting.

Unreimbursed medical expenses (which include the cost of the assisted living facility) can be considered to help qualify the assisted living facility resident in receiving Aid and Attendance. The monthly payments from Aid and Attendance will help to pay the cost of the assisted living facility. Because of that, Aid and Attendance benefits can sometimes eliminate the need to apply for Medicaid – for some assisted living residents.

Furthermore, the extra income from a VA Aid and Assistance Pension can amount to a considerable amount of monthly cash: An additional $1,094 for a surviving spouse, up to $1,703 a month for a single veteran, or up to $ 2,019 a month for a couple (12/1/11 figures.) Under some circumstances, a family member may receive this stipend as a non-licensed in-home attendant. Your advisor will help you determine whether or not that is possible. A good source of information can be found at the local Veterans of Foreign Wars chapter or the American Legion.

Who Qualifies for Non-Service Connected Benefits?

Before you can begin to seek the non-service connected benefits, you need to know what the Veteran's Administration defines as being a veteran. For most people this designation is clear, but if you are unclear about any of the benefits, seeking out the support of the VA will be helpful in answering your questions.

You might also want to go to an aid organization which can help you navigate the tricky world of benefits. They are often free and can allow you to focus on your health as opposed to the money you require.

A veteran can qualify for non-service connected veteran benefits if the veteran:

- meets the basic 90-day rule of active service
- served at least one day during a time of war
- is permanently disabled
- meets certain asset and income criteria
- discharge is other than dishonorable

It can help to understand these terms a bit better to know for certain if you qualify or not.

The basic 90-day rule of active service means that you need to have been called up for serving and then been a part of active service for those 90 days. However, veterans who enlisted after September 7, 1980 will need to have served for at least 24 months in total or for the total period for which they were called up — i.e. National Reserves and/or the National Guard.

Thus, if you were deployed for a three-year period, this would cover you for active service, assuming you had one day during a war time. However, if you were only called up for 90 days, this too would count for the requirement.

Serving for one day during a war does not mean that you were necessarily in active fighting; it just means that you were on active duty, and that you might have been called up to the front lines at some point. You do not need to have actively fought against an enemy during this one-day period.

Your discharge from service must have been other than dishonorable to secure these benefits. When you are dishonorably discharged, you may not take advantage of these pension benefits.

As with other benefits, you will need to prove that you are permanently disabled to secure the Improved Pension. This is a process which begins with your physician submitting your medical records and assessing your current physical condition. If they determine you are unable to go back to work and that you are unable to perform your everyday duties without help, you may be listed as permanently disabled.

Once you have had a medical examination and you have gathered the medical history, you will need to submit these files to the Veteran's Administration for review. At that time, they will determine whether they too consider you to be permanently disabled or if they need further assessment to make their determination.

Surviving spouses may also be eligible for the Improved Pension if their spouses served in these war periods:

- World War II: December 7, 1941 to December 31, 1946.
- Korean War: June 27, 1950 to January 31, 1955.
- Vietnam War: August 5, 1964 to May 7, 1975. Veterans who served "in country" begin this war period on February 28, 1961.

- Gulf War: August 2, 1990, through a date which is to be set by the law of Presidential Proclamation.

There are certain income and asset limitations which determine the amount of money you can receive as a part of the Improved Pension plan. A veteran who has a higher income or asset level may not be able to secure as high of a pension payment.

The Levels of Improved Pension

Within the Improved Pension program are three levels in which the veteran may be able to have benefits.

- Basic
- Housebound
- Aid and Attendance

Basic Level

What many people don't realize is that the basic level of the Improved Pension does not require that you are physically disabled. You can also be suffering from a mental condition as a result of your service or as a condition which developed after following the service guidelines as listed.

The benefit amounts for the Basic Level are:

- A veteran alone – $ 12,256 per year.
- A veteran with a dependent – $16,051 per year.
- A surviving spouse – $7933 per year.
- A surviving spouse with a dependent – $10,385 per year.

The basic financial criteria which a veteran has to meet to be able to receive pension at the basic level include:

- A veteran has countable income of less than the pension amount. The countable income is the income that a veteran or their surviving spouse might receive in a year. But this total is determined after health care costs are deducted.

- A veteran does not have enough money to support himself or herself for the rest of his/her life, as determined by the VA.
- The primary residence and vehicles are not used in the assessment of net worth.

Those veterans who qualify for the pension will need to fill out form 21-526. Surviving spouses would need to fill out form 21-534.

Housebound Level

There are some veterans whose disabilities prevent them from performing everyday duties on their own. These veterans might need help from medical professionals or home health aides.

Surviving spouses of veterans who are housebound can also receive benefits.

The benefit amounts for the Housebound Level are:

- A veteran alone — $14,978 per year.
- A veteran with a dependent — $18,733 per year.

- A surviving spouse — $9,696 per year.
- A surviving spouse with a dependent — $12,144 per year.

The financial criteria for those who are housebound still applies:

- A veteran has countable income of less than the pension amount. The countable income is the income that a veteran or their surviving spouse might receive in a year. But this total is determined after health care costs are deducted.
- A veteran does not have enough money to support themselves for the rest of their lives, as determined by the VA.
- The primary residence and vehicles are not used in the assessment of net worth.

Those veterans with a physical condition will need to have this condition verified by a physician before benefits will be dispensed.

Aid and Attendance Level

A veteran who is disabled, fits the regular pension criteria, and who might need assistance in the home (though they need not be bedridden or in an assisted living facility or in a home health care program) may qualify for the Aid and Attendance level of pension.

This payment will be in addition to other pensions which you might receive to help support the person who needs assistance. This benefit will NOT be in addition to a Housebound pension, just in addition to the basic pension.

A physical will need to confirm the level of the disability before this pension will be distributed. What makes this level different is that the physician must also show that the condition of the veteran or the surviving spouse has deteriorated to the point where they need daily assistance.

The same financial criteria apply at this level too:

- A veteran has countable income of less than the pension amount.
- The countable income is the income that a veteran or their surviving spouse might receive in a year. But this total is determined after health care costs are deducted.
- A veteran does not have enough money to support themselves for the rest of their lives, as determined by the VA.
- The primary residence and vehicles are not used in the assessment of net worth.

These are the current financial benefit levels available for Aid and Attendance as of January 2012:

- A veteran alone — $20,447 per year.

- A veteran with one dependent – $24,239 per year.
- Two veterans married to each other – $31,578 per year.
- Surviving spouse of a veteran –$13,138 per year.

Determining Countable Income

While countable income has already been defined, it may be necessary to explain this in more detail to avoid confusion.

Countable income includes:

- A part of the income of a dependent.
- Disability payments.
- Interest.
- Dividends.
- Net income from farming or another home business.

What is NOT included in countable income:

- SSI – Supplemental Security Income.
- Food stamps.
- Welfare benefits.

You can determine countable income on your own.

Example: Tom is a veteran who has proven that he has a physical disability. He is applying for the pension, but there is some debate over how much of his income will be factored into the final determination.

If Tom makes about $15,000 a year from Social Security, but his wife, Margaret, earns $8,000 a year from Social Security, then they have some income coming in annually. Margaret also earns about $5,000 each year after retiring from a small greeting card company and receiving a pension.

This adds up to $28,000 in *income*.

Net worth: Tom and Margaret only have $35,000 in savings and in CDs, plus they bought their house a long time ago.

Expenses: Each month, Tom pays for Margaret's physical therapy, which amounts to $1,500.

The couple's Medicare premiums are around $200 a month.

Margaret carries supplemental insurance for the couple, at $100 each month.

All of this adds up to $1,800 per month, or $21,600 a year.

You need to take the expenses from the income, or:

$28,000 - $21,600 = $6,400. This would be the countable income.

Since the maximum pension one can receive is $24,239 (at the basic level for a veteran with a dependent), the couple is eligible to receive up to $17,839 per year:

$24,239 - $6,400 = $17,839.

While this might not seem like a large sum of money, this can help to make ends meet in a household which doesn't have a lot of savings.

How to Prove Aid and Assistance Needs

The first thing one needs to do in order obtain Aid and Assistance is to prove they qualify for the pension. Once this is complete, then they need to show that their situation includes one of the following circumstances:

- The veteran is bedridden and must stay in bed to continue his or her treatment.
- The veteran requires assistance from someone else to perform daily tasks – i.e. changing their clothes, bathing, etc.
- The veteran is in an assisted living facility or nursing home.
- The veteran is blind.

These situations can be proved with medical documentation which will be sent to the VA upon applying for the benefits. The medical records should be as detailed as possible to show specifically what the veteran can and what they cannot do for themselves.

Can You Receive Service Connected and Non-Service Connected Benefits at the Same Time?

While you might qualify for both benefits, according to the guidelines of the VA, it is not possible to receive both benefit payments. What you will receive is the larger payment of the two, and you can submit a form for both of the benefits to insure you get the highest pension possible.

How Does a Surviving Spouse Qualify for the Veteran's Pension?

A surviving spouse will qualify for non-service connected benefits, like a pension, if the veteran fulfilled all of their service requirements and the spouse must have married the veteran within fifteen years after the service when the injury occurred.

The spouse must also have stayed married to the spouse for at least one year or more after a child was born in the marriage or if the child was born before the marriage.

How Will A Veteran's Pension Affect SSI and Medicaid Eligibility?

While each state might have their own ideas about how a veteran's pension might affect SSI and Medicaid, it's generally accepted that the SSI payment is going to be less than the basic pension amounts.

However, in the case of a surviving spouse, if their VA pension is less than the federal SSI, then they would be eligible to receive both payments, though they would only receive some of the SSI amount, not necessarily the full amount.

There are a number of benefits available to veterans who have been afflicted with disabilities, even if the injury was not the result of a war time effort. Looking into these benefits will allow a veteran to receive additional compensation for their commitment to the military, while also helping to provide them with support when they need it most.

CHAPTER 9

Life Care Planning

Life care planning, a relatively new practice area, delivers to you or your loved one a more holistic approach to elder care that goes beyond just the legal issues addressed by elder law.

Traditional elder law focuses on estate planning, legal strategies designed to preserve assets, and probate avoidance. Life care planning goes beyond legal and financial concerns and addresses the physical, psychological and social aspects of elder care.

A life care planning attorney can help a client through the many pitfalls associated with a voluntary life change. Of course, if the person is suddenly struck with disability, the life care attorney is an invaluable help to the client's family. A life care attorney is also a fail-safe for the client who may not have a family upon which to rely. If there are no other reasons to enlist the services of such a person, these two are crucial.

The Benefits of Life Care Planning

Life care planning has several important goals. In the first stage of the life care planning process, the elder's total care needs (physical, psychological and social) are assessed by qualified staff, often called geriatric care managers. This enables the attorney to take immediate steps to help the elder maintain independence in the community, wherever possible and for as long as possible, before considering other living arrangements. Chapter 11 discusses the roles of geriatric care managers, and how to select the right one for your situation.

Typically, health care problems like Alzheimer's, strokes, or mobility issues are among the biggest barriers to the elder maintaining a high quality of life and independence. Life care planning focuses a team of specialists on slowing down deterioration through the efforts of home health care nurses and/or aides, physical therapists, recreational therapists, day treatment programs and the like.

The life care plan also identifies any additional benefits for which the elder may be eligible, such as Veterans Benefits, additional Medicare benefits, or any Medicaid benefits. By attempting to slow down the elder's decline and helping the elder maintain a more independent environment, surprisingly enough, everyone saves money. This happens because the elder remains in a less expensive and less restrictive environment, compared to assisted living or a skilled nursing facility.

Within a life care plan can be information about how insurance will be handled and what insurance options are available for various care needs. Instead of having to scramble to figure out how to handle insurance, this can be drawn up into the plan for future reference.

A life care planning attorney can be a significant source of education and information to the elder and his or her family. In addition to identifying the available care resources to support the elder, an experienced life care planning attorney (with a geriatric care manager on board) can assist the elder with the many types of care options available to the elder.

While a main goal of life care planning is care coordination, another important goal is elder advocacy – designed to protect the rights of the elderly. An attorney is often in a much better position to be an advocate for the elder compared to other professional service providers. Attorneys are required to know the law, and attorneys are often in the best position to hold people accountable and thereby protect the rights of the elderly client.

Additional goals of a life care planning attorney include providing the elder with peace of mind and support as they age. People will be able to state their wishes ahead of any impairment. An experienced life care planning attorney has a large pool of elder care resources from which to draw, and this empowers the elder and his/her family in confronting the challenges associated with aging.

Relaying Information to Family Members

One key to a successful life care plan is the communication that takes place between the elderly person and his or her family.

While death and aging are often considered taboo subjects in today's culture, the truth is that these issues can affect more than just the elderly person when the topic is avoided. As seniors age, a number of legal, financial and lifestyle elements of their lives and their family's lives will change, causing considerable trouble if careful planning is not undertaken.

By sitting down with loved ones as soon as possible, together the family can make decisions for health care and estate management before the elderly person becomes ill or passes on. A Power or Attorney may be granted to a family member who is trusted by the elder to make important decisions on their behalf. Family members will know what to do during health events or other developments. Families in conflict will not have anything over which to argue as the plans are already in place

Aging with dignity is the goal of any life care planning arrangement. In taking care of the details now, a person can focus on making the most of their later years. A life care plan allows not only the elder to be content with their life and with the way they age, but the children and other loved ones will not have to worry about what they will need to step in to do. With a life care plan, there are no surprises and the elder can focus on more important things — like staying healthy and active as long as possible.

Choosing Alternatives for Senior Living

One of the biggest challenges families face is long-term placement in a nursing home. Should nursing home confinement become necessary, a life care planning attorney would assist with restructuring the elder's assets. This can help the elder qualify for Medicaid at the earliest possible time, which usually saves a substantial amount of money.

Furthermore, a durable power of attorney must be established before a senior becomes incapacitated; this is an important part of life care planning that will preserve the senior's assets and the entire family's peace of mind. A life care attorney would already have set up a durable power of attorney for himself or a relative, so the situation described in the earlier example of Frederik (Chapter 7) would not occur.

Even more, the life care attorney would have at his or her disposal all the options for housing that are available to the client. The life care attorney will understand the various living arrangements in light of the client's needs and desires — and thus make a series of recommendations for a good match.

Example: Phyllis has been a life care client of Attorney Smith since her husband, a World War II veteran, died 8 years ago. She is an extremely independent and healthy 80-year-old from Daytona Beach who loves to garden. She also possesses a lovely home full of memorabilia from her travels and her family.

Attorney Smith knows she cannot afford an assisted living facility that offers gardening and a large apartment. He also knows of an extremely well run, owner-occupied manufactured home community in her city which can provide these advantages. He privately doubts, as well, that Phyllis would tolerate restrictions on closing hours and visiting hours typical of alternative housing.

With his help, Phyllis sells her home and buys a three-bedroom, relatively new mobile home for $89,000 in an owner-occupied park. Her homeowners rent includes television, utilities, and maintenance of common areas, and is fixed at $400 monthly. She has only to add her telephone charges. As in an assisted living facility, she will enjoy at her complex many activities and games and trips to plays and theatres. She will have a weekly bridge game and the park has a heated pool and gym. She can still cook and entertain her family for meals, if she chooses. Her grandchildren can visit for extended periods. She appreciates the freedom and advantages of the larger quarters. The Park van can take her shopping and to doctors' and dentists' appointments.

If Phyllis becomes incapacitated, Attorney Smith knows she is eligible for a Veteran's Administration Aid and Attendance Pension because of her late husband's service. In addition, her family or her attorney can arrange, with the diagnosis from a doctor, for her to be accepted into a local hospice for doctors' and nurses' visits. Phyllis can end her days surrounded by friends, her memorabilia, and her family.

As you can see, a life care planning attorney can assess the many options available to the elder whom he knows well. The attorney can advise about differing assisted living facilities, explaining their advantages and disadvantages to the client. Those who have set out to determine the best course for themselves are often met by a bewildering array of choices; often they settle on a particular place because they know someone there, and become disillusioned after they have settled in.

Many facilities greet the investigating elder with a salesperson who stresses the amenities of the facility and may receive a commission for enrolling residents. Only later, does the elder learn of restrictions and rules that he/she may not endorse.

In the next chapter, we take a close look at several alternative housing choices that are available to Florida seniors.

CHAPTER 10

Alternative Housing Choices: Another Way of Protecting Assets

Often, an elder is placed in a skilled nursing facility after a fall or a stroke or heart attack, and then recommended to assisted living. Help can be had outside an institution, preserving in many cases the individual's assets.

One example of a low-cost but satisfactory option is a retirement park such as Del Webb's Sun City. The park outside of Tampa has been the living quarters for several years' worth of elders. With a reception center and individual small houses, duplexes, and apartments, these "villages" as they are called offer golf courses, swimming pools, and activities such as ballroom dancing and crafts. Many of these communities, such as the granddaddy Sun City outside of Phoenix, Arizona, offer hospitals and compassionate care for the dying.

Example: Sylvia, a former Broadway actress and dancer of the '40s, is moved by her daughter from a depressing living situation to an apartment, where she fares little better. A brother in Tampa arranges for Sylvia to buy a small home in Sun City, where she is encouraged to mingle and is eventually urged to teach dance. By doing the latter, she becomes acquainted with several long-term residents. Although in her 80's, Sylvia is spry enough to join the Sun City cheerleading squad, where she has a real place in the community. Friends who make the drive to visit are amazed at her transformation.

Because these communities require less capital outlay than an assisted living facility, and because they offer more freedom and flexibility, they are often the choice of the retiring elder.

Retirement villages patterned after the Sun City model (but much more expensive) are being built around eastern Central Florida communities such as Clermont, and often in Arizona. Model homes demonstrate amenities in keeping with the most exclusive of assisted living facilities, which are combined with the privacy and spaciousness of a manufactured home. These homes, however, are site-built and made to withstand Florida hurricanes.

The choice for many affluent retirees, these communities have clubhouses, swimming pools, even restaurants and woodworking shops. Hardly a hobby or interest cannot be explored in these communities. The caliber of the people living in them, mostly professionals and executives, are comparable to those in the most desirable assisted living facilities. A factor to consider is the ownership of these "villages." Often, a national homebuilding chain is the sponsor, turning the place over to the owners or Homeowners' Association at a specific, sold-out point. Potential buyers should be familiar with these options.

Example: Harold, a retired engineer, and Jeannie, his journalist wife, sell their New Jersey home for a large sum and wish to live near their oldest friend Tom in Clermont, Florida. They have been visiting Tom for several years and going on trips with him, and have grown to love his scenic part of Central Florida. To their delight, they find two upscale "villages" on nearby acres which compete in amenities and expense for the two healthy and interesting 67-year-olds.

After extensive investigation, in concert with local resident Tom, they choose their home and lot, and travel during the three-month wait for the home's completion. Upon moving in, Jeannie works as a volunteer on the village newspaper and participates daily in a water aerobics class. Harold joins a group in the woodworking shop and learns to carve small wood figures, a hobby he has always wanted to pursue.

An Even More Convenient Choice

As in the example of Phyllis, the independent Daytona Beach retiree (Chapter 9), there is often the option of moving to a manufactured home (mobile home) park in the elder's community. This may be less of an ordeal than moving to one of the Sun City villages and will be far less expensive than signing up with a newer, senior site-built village.

An extremely wide variety of these parks exists in Florida. They range from the expensive and new to the moderate-priced and old, and almost all types can be found in the retiree's vicinity. While the public perception of the hurricane-ravaged mobile home park is true of a few older facilities, the newer homes (since 1980) have been anchored and built to withstand these storms. Much bad press has resulted from mobile home devastation in seaside communities of an older vintage. The buyer has to be aware of tie downs and foundations, just as he has to know the difference between rental parks and owner-occupied parks.

To differentiate, a rental park is owned and controlled by an individual or a consortium. The owners, like apartment dwellers, do not control their monthly expenses. The coach is bought and sold, but the lot remains the property of the landlord. Lot rents can escalate tremendously, but there must be a clause in the park's rules and regulations which explains caps and dues.

In contrast, an owner-occupied park is one in which the buyer purchases coach and lot, much as with a site-built home. Frequently, park residents are in the process of buying their own parks from a landlord; in cases like these there is a buy-in.

Example: Letty and John, a newly-retired couple in Altamonte Springs, Florida wish to spend their healthy elder years traveling in their motor home and vacationing in their jointly owned timeshare apartments. Because they know these activities will use much of their retirement income, they settle on buying an older, anchored coach in an owner-occupied park in Leesburg, Florida. They sell their large home, invest in a coach for less than a fifth of their capital, and use the remainder to invest for their travel.

While their living situation is not unimportant to them, it is less important than having discretionary income. With their Social Security checks and the interest on their investments, Letty and John are able to spend several months a year seeing the country and visiting old friends. For them, a small investment in retirement living is the right one.

Because they come into the park as it is being bought, Letty and John must pay a buy-in. They have already set aside a large sum for that purpose. In their case, with 144 homes in the park each paying a monthly stipend toward the loan, they must catch up, or pay a lump sum equal to what established owners have paid. For Letty and John, the buy-in is $16,000. From closing on, they will be charged $139 a month as their share of retiring the loan on the property. Even with paying that sum, their monthly expenses will rarely exceed $400 for utilities, funds for contingencies, and maintenance.

Reverse Mortgage

An option that has come into wide use in recent times is applying for a reverse mortgage from the Federal Government. Videos explaining the process are available for no charge, and the program is based on escalating home value. Because home value is under pressure, these rules may change; the upshot is that the retiree lacking (or wishing to preserve) income can receive a payment enabling them to stay put with certain legal restrictions.

Again, the senior must investigate the latest rulings concerning this program; he must be advised that, as of 2009, mobile home dwellers were not eligible for this program unless the homes met certain standards, such as permanent foundations. State rules may apply as well. Since there are many issues to consider with a reverse mortgage, it is important to seek the guidance of an elder attorney who can explain the process to you, and help you decide if this is an appropriate strategy.

Apartments and Condominiums

Sometimes, an elder will retire and downsize to some kind of intermediate living facility for economic or social reasons. In such cases, condominiums to rent and buy abound in Florida; also, apartment facilities are plentiful. Floridians are fortunate in the variety and abundance of these living choices.

With apartments and condominiums, retirees can experience all of the comforts and the privacy of home, while also being adjacent to others in similar situations. Within these communities, adults can interact and create social networks which can support the health and well-being of all.

However, it must be noted that apartments and condominiums are unable to provide all of the medical services that assisted living and nursing home facilities can provide. Thus, if a resident is unable to care for himself or herself, these apartments and condominiums may not be the best choice.

Example: Bill, a department head, retires from a local university just as his wife of 50 years dies. Rather than making a permanent move to an assisted living facility, he decides to temporarily relocate to an apartment near his son's home in Longwood, Florida with all his notes and papers to write a textbook. He takes meals and trips with his son and his family and gradually recovers from the loss of his wife while he writes, daily, on a lifetime of materials. When the book and grieving are finished, he plans to live in a Winter Park, Florida retirement facility which houses many of his former colleagues.

A Long-Distance Change

In this transient time, when more and more people chase a different climate or a different culture, it happens that retirees move to Mexico or Guatemala, where their Social Security checks can buy them luxury; or California, where the climate is agreeable after a series of hot, humid Florida summers.

Example: Leslie, a Florida editor, is forced to retire when her newspaper is sold to a new owner. Leslie is widowed. At the age of 60, she has ample savings and Social Security to make a long-distance move. She favors Southern California, a part of the country she has always loved. Her daughter lives there, as well.

First, Leslie consults her younger friends who have been caretakers for their own parents. They advise her to move while she is young enough to make new friends so she is not entirely dependent upon her daughter, who has many obligations of her own. She then goes on the internet to find a city in Southern California which is not too large but which boasts of excellent climate. She settles on Vista, California, an exurban San Diego town of 71,000; this city is also 27 miles from her daughter's home in Fallbrook, California.

Leslie flies out to visit the area and to her delight finds seven senior mobile home parks for residents 55 and older. She finds two which are owner-occupied and buys a coach for $60,000 with a $27,000 buy-in for the ownership stipend. Satisfied she will have an agreeable living situation, Leslie returns to Florida. She sells and gives away her furnishings, loads up her car with her treasured art and some memorabilia, ships her papers ahead by UPS, and drives with a friend across country, stopping to see areas in Texas, Nevada, Arizona, and Eastern California before arriving in Vista. Leslie then buys an airplane ticket and sends her friend home. Cost of the move: $1000, including the ticket.

At the local Salvation Army, Leslie buys furnishings for her home for under $1000, and then recoups the price by selling an article about the move and her new furniture. She makes friends in the park, in her church, and in a local club and eventually sees her daughter only monthly and calls on her very infrequently for favors. After a time, she meets a widower and marries.

Seniors have a broad range of housing options, each based upon their care needs and their budget. Alternative housing and elder communities provide opportunities that allow seniors to progress from independent living to assisted living, and nursing home care.

CHAPTER 11

The Role of Geriatric Care Managers and How to Select Them

Having someone to help in managing the care of an elderly relative can mean the difference between a life of chaos and a life of calm reassurance. With the use of a geriatric care manager, families can navigate the often confusing waters of the health care system. These professionals can also help families and their loved ones adapt to the challenges aging can present on a near daily basis.

With training in many areas of elder care and health management, geriatric care managers help families help themselves. While many decisions rest in the hands of the families, this does not necessarily mean the families are ready to handle such important and life-changing decisions. Often, the family is emotionally involved with the process, which only makes some decisions unclear. Instead of approaching decisions with limited experience and a clear bias in the situation, geriatric care managers are employed to be the friend of the family in a difficult time.

What a Geriatric Care Manager Does

The idea of geriatric care management is something which has become all the more important as people begin to live longer lives. With the increase in health technology, people are not only living healthier lives, but also they are exceeding life expectancies by decades.

Decisions which were once unheard of are now becoming everyday occurrences — much to the confusion of families and of hospitals. While hospitals want to do what is right for their patients, they may not have the consent of the families.

That's where the geriatric care manager will step in.

Geriatric care management can be defined as a system in which elderly care is coordinated and planned to maintain or to improve the quality of life of the elderly person. For example, an elderly person may want to stay at home, taking care of themselves and a loved one for as long as possible. However, without sufficient resources, the elderly person may not be able to complete all of the tasks necessary to maintain their health and their home.

Example: Suzanne's mother, Wilma, has been living in her home for the last 10 years by herself after Suzanne's father passed away from cancer. Though Wilma's health is strong, she has troubles with arthritis, which can make moving around the home difficult for her and often errands are difficult as well.

Instead of turning to Suzanne for help, Wilma often makes do without necessary items or misses doctor's appointments.

A geriatric care manager can help to promote the home care that Suzanne needs, allowing her to continue living in her home, with the support of someone who is able to run errands for her or to help her get to her necessary appointments.

The Geriatric Care Manager's Qualifications

When selecting a geriatric care manager, families will want to look for professionals who have a set of qualifications that include:

- Degree
- License
- Certification

Many states will have different requirements for those who call themselves geriatric care managers. Ideally, those looking for the services of a geriatric care manager will want to find someone who is not only a Registered Nurse, but also someone who has completed some sort of training as a Certified Care Manager.

With the health background and the care management background, the geriatric care manager will be able to easily assess multiple areas of the client's life to determine what needs to be done to help support their goals and lifestyle.

That said, geriatric care managers should also be trained in the specific issues of aging and gerontology. This will allow the manager to make decisions based on the specific needs of the elderly.

In addition, a background that includes training in social work, therapy, and counseling can also help the geriatric care manager have a broader scope and perspective on the needs of their clients.

The Numerous Jobs of the Care Manager

In the role of a geriatric care manager, there are numerous tasks the professional can handle for their clients, including:

- Assessing the needs of the client
- Creating individual care plans
- Determining the eligibility for assistance
- Referring to other specialists
- Assisting in transitions from one living situation to another

- Providing intervention during a crisis situation
- Communicating with relatives who are out of town

Of course, with each client, the needs can change, often expanding beyond this list and beyond the limitations of the geriatric care manager's background.

Better put, the care manager often has to think outside of the box, finding solutions to problems which they may not have learned about in school, but which they can certainly handle with their experience.

Example: John did not want to move into the nursing home and was frustrated when his children decided this move was the best idea for him.

As a result, John began to cause trouble at the nursing home. In fact, he attempted a few escapes from the facility with the help of one son who was sympathetic to his needs.

However, this son did not have any legal right to make decisions for his father. This resulted in the son becoming estranged from the rest of the family.

With the help of a geriatric care manager, the family was able to sit down together and discuss a solution that would benefit John. The family listened to all sides of the argument, eventually agreeing to an arrangement to move John into a senior center which was more to his liking.

Many people find that the help of a geriatric care manager is most helpful when a parent or relative becomes too much of a burden.

While a family member might feel guilty about handing over what they assume to be their responsibility, the guidance and service of a professional geriatric care manager is more helpful than they might realize. In fact, seniors may actually be more forthcoming with a care manager about embarrassing or distressful life issues than they would be with family members.

The time families spend trying to navigate the confusing system of elder care might be better spent visiting with their relative, either on the phone or in person. The details of the senior person's care can then be left in the hands of a trusted individual who understands who to call and when to call them during times of health issues or in times of other crises.

Creating a Care Plan for a Loved One

The key to helping an elderly relative is to ensure that care is given before it becomes vitally necessary – better put, the elderly relative needs to be assessed for physical, mental and emotional health, before the time comes when they cannot ask for help themselves.

Within many elderly people is a need to maintain independence for the long term – and to refrain from asking for help from others. Asking for help is often thought of as a sign of weakness and a sign that the elderly person may not be able to stay in their home anymore.

However, this is not the case in today's resourceful times.

When a person has an elderly relative, it is a good idea to check in with this relative often to see how they are doing. The relative should be looking for signs of trouble, such as:

- Health problems
- Confusion
- Memory loss
- Signs of dementia or Alzheimer's

It is especially important to keep watch for signs of trouble in those who may have a history of health problems or who have relatives with dementia and other age-related disorders.

Many conditions can now be managed with therapy and with medication, but only if the conditions are caught early.

If signs of trouble are seen in a loved one, it may be time to talk to the elderly person's primary care doctor as well as a geriatric care manager to begin the process of evaluating their health, including assessing:

- physical health
- mental health
- the ability to perform daily tasks
- medication schedule adherence
- living arrangements

This assessment process can be handled by a geriatric care manager who will visit with the elderly person to determine whether he or she needs further help from others to maintain a healthy and happy life.

Once the problems are uncovered in the life of the elderly person, the geriatric care manager can then determine what steps need to be taken to support the client in any way possible.

Regular check-ins can then be scheduled to determine if the elderly client needs more or less support as the care plan is activated and family communication is established.

Maintaining Independence in the Long Term

Creating the circumstances for an elderly person to continue their way of life is a multi-faceted project. The first step is to assess the individual's needs in terms of care, and from there, a care plan can be created.

There are a number of different services which may need to be incorporated into the person's life:

- Home care services
- Housing
- Socialization programs
- Legal planning
- Financial planning
- Transportation

Within each of these services are even more details to consider, based on the needs of each individual person. In the past, elder care was a more structured system in which a person either went to a nursing home or they did not. Today, a geriatric care manager can evaluate on a case-by-case basis to determine the unique needs of an individual.

Home care services. For many elderly people, the idea of going into a hospital or a nursing home is not desirable. They want to stay in their homes where they are comfortable and where they feel safe.

For people who do not have immediate health needs, this desire can be accommodated with the help of a geriatric care manager. This professional will work with home health care providers to arrange regular visits or ongoing support, depending on the health needs.

Often, this sort of care can complement regular doctor visits, when coordinated with the person's primary care physician or specialists. However, regular appointments and testing will still be necessary outside of the home.

Housing. As some elderly people may have trouble securing housing or navigating the housing market due to a lack of resources (i.e. family members in the local area, finances, etc.), a geriatric care manager can help with these tasks as well.

By working with the client to find adequate housing, the care manager will help to establish a secure living arrangement in which the client's needs can still be met. Various housing possibilities include an assisted living center, senior citizen apartment/condominium centers, or other housing as deemed suitable for the particular client.

Socialization programs. One of the bigger problems of elderly people is the isolation they encounter on a regular basis. When a person is unable to leave their home due to physical restrictions, they can often feel alone and depressed, which can lead to an increased risk of health problems.

As a result, socialization programs for the elderly have been created with their clients in mind. Senior centers have begun to be more prevalent in larger cities, while volunteers can also come to a person's house to sit with them and to continue the social interaction seniors need to stay mentally sharp and mentally engaged.

Legal planning. As a person becomes older, their affairs may seem to become simpler, but in reality this is far from the case. Estate planning, legal wills, power of attorney, and other legal actions need the advice and the guidance of a qualified legal professional.

With the help of a life care planning attorney, an elderly citizen will be able to manage their finances, property, and tax questions long before the end of their lives. This can assure their families that after death, the person's life is in order and that the remaining survivors do not have to tie up loose ends.

Financial planning. Since many adults are living longer than expected, their retirement funds and plans may not be up to speed with their longevity. To help an elderly person manage their finances, a geriatric care manager will step in and either work with the client directly or they may refer the client to a planner who is skilled in handling the finances of senior citizens.

This financial planning will allow the senior the opportunity to not only have enough money for their basic needs and health care, but also for the things they longed to afford and to enjoy after they retired.

Transportation. Some elderly citizens can have difficulty getting from their home to doctor's appointments or to general errands. In managing transportation, geriatric care managers can ensure that their clients are able to do the tasks and errands they need to do, without necessarily relying on their families for support.

Choosing the Right Geriatric Care Manager

What many families find when they begin the search for a geriatric care manager is that their choices are overwhelming.

Not only are many care managers readily available, but knowing what they might need from them can be just as perplexing. Not knowing how many services they might need and how they might pay for them is a complicated matter.

However, there are a few basic rules a loved one can follow to find the best geriatric care manager possible for their needs and for the needs of their elderly relative.

Check Certifications. Though it might seem like common sense to look into the certification of the professionals one hires to care for a relative, many people simply assume a professional is who they say they are.

When selecting a geriatric care manager, one should be certain to check the status of all certifications by requesting copies of the certifications or diplomas and then calling the boards that granted the certifications. Any out-of-date licenses or certifications should be reason for concern.

Learn about Medicaid's Limitations. Though Medicaid is of great help with many costs for taking care of an elderly person, there are limitations. It is in the best interest of everyone involved to learn as much as possible about Medicaid and about how it can help the client get what they need.

Often, a geriatric care manager will also be able to help here, but having a general understanding ahead of time will allow the family to know what they can reasonably expect from a care manager. A life care planning attorney will be able to specifically identify – and facilitate the process of applying for – any Medicaid benefits for which the elder may be eligible, as well as available Veterans Benefits or any Medicare benefits.

Talk with the Primary Care Doctor. Often, a primary care doctor for an elderly person will be able to refer families to geriatric care managers; they will also be able to let a family know when it might be time to hire such a professional.

Regular doctor appointments will help to keep the person assessed at regular intervals, allowing the family to have a clear idea as to when it might be time for care management.

Look for Experience. While the certifications of a geriatric care manager are important, so is the experience level of the professional. Often, a care manager who has had more experience with the elderly is going to be able to give better advice and have access to better resources within the community.

Newer care managers can be helpful, but when an elderly care situation is complicated, experience should outweigh the number of certifications on a resume.

Consider the Pricing Terms. As elderly support services are often priced on a per-service basis, a geriatric care manager will also charge depending on the services they arrange and the support they give.

One should check ahead of time to see what insurances a geriatric care manager might be able to use in their arrangement services, while also checking to see what the geriatric care manager charges for their time.

A geriatric care manager can be a lifesaver for a family who has little or no idea how to handle an elderly relative. By stepping in to help with the details of aging and the issues that come along with aging, a professional geriatric care manager helps to create a sense of peace for families.

As a result, an elderly relative can have the well-being they deserve in their later years, as opposed to struggling to be healthy, happy, and supported.

CHAPTER 12

How to Select
an Assisted Living Facility (ALF)

Assisted living may become a part of an elder's care plan as they age. While a small number of these care centers may have had a poor reputation in the past, the centers of today are far more modern and often relatively comparable to living at home.

By providing assistance to the elderly residents who live there, assisted living facilities can help the resident feel as though they are maintaining a semblance of their former lives. The resident can also feel safe with any medical conditions that may need to be monitored.

Also known as adult retirement homes, continuing care communities, and retirement communities or personal care homes, these facilities can provide a watchful eye for those adults who might need more monitoring than other elderly residents might.

Many of these assisted living facilities are currently covered by Medicaid, though others have lost their ties to Medicaid coverage. Checking with the facility ahead of time can allow a family to see which facilities may be more cost-effective.

What Is an Assisted Living Facility?

An assisted living facility is a residence that offers an intermediate level of care appropriate for many seniors. They can help monitor the care of elderly residents who need assistance with the Activities of Daily Living (ADLs), yet who wish to live as independently as possible. These facilities can supervise the residents as well as help them with:

- The administration of medication
- Basic health needs
- Personal care tasks

Unlike the typical nursing homes that many elderly people try to avoid residing in, these facilities work more like a traditional housing facility, but with the support staff on hand to deal with age-related issues.

Some of the things a resident can expect from an assisted living facility include:

- A trained medical expert available during certain hours
- A staff who can handle basic needs and tasks
- Private apartment-like housing for each resident or couple
- Common areas for socializing with other residents
- Communal eating in some facilities

A definition for an assisted living facility is not nationally recognized. Therefore, the burden is on the family of the client to thoroughly check out each facility before signing an agreement to send a loved one to live at such a facility. A geriatric care manager can be a great source of help to families when evaluating ALFs.

Residents who might be well suited to the assisted living facility experience include seniors who do not have major medical issues that need constant monitoring. Unlike nursing homes, the assisted living organizations will not have medical equipment on hand. There might be nurses who come in to provide basic care, but long-term and chronic diseases may require more extensive care than an ALF can provide.

A good candidate for an assisted living facility is one who can manage to move around on their own, even with help from a motorized scooter or other mobility devices. This person might be able to live on their own, but may have issues with:

- Isolation
- Trouble with medication management
- Everyday tasks like shopping and cleaning

Questions to Ask the Assisted Living Facility Staff

Since the burden of proving that an assisted living facility is up to the task of caring for its residents lies solely on the residents and their families, it's a good idea to ask a number of questions before signing up a loved one for this sort of residence. Some of the questions one might want to ask include:

- Does the facility have a current license from the state?
- Is there a formal quality assurance program in place?
- Who is on the staff and what are their certifications?
- Is the staff expected to continue training and maintain their licenses?
- What services are provided to the residents?
- What should residents NOT expect to find at the facility?
- What problems have occurred in the past?
- Have there been any complaints?
- How much can the family be involved in the planning process of the resident's care?
- What will happen in an emergency?
- What activities will a resident enjoy?
- What are the costs associated with living at this facility?
- Is Medicaid an insurance which can cover some costs?

- If the Medicaid status is taken away from the facility, what happens to the resident?
- What handicap accessibility features are in place?
- What meals are available to the residents, should they choose to use that service?
- How long is the waiting list for the facility?
- A prospective client and their family should also be certain to tour the building to make sure it fits their needs as well as their personal comfort levels.

This is a facility in which an elderly person will be spending a majority of their time. For this reason, comfort isn't just something to be desired; it is something to be expected right from the start. If the resident isn't comfortable where they are living, this can affect not only their physical health, but also their emotional state.

Safety

Safety should be a primary concern of both the resident who is applying to live in an assisted living facility as well as of the family member who takes part in the process of determining where their family member will live. Safety issues that should be discussed prior to signing any paperwork for the facility include:

- What happens during a medical emergency?
- How fast can help be summoned?
- Is the property protected from outside intruders?
- What safety features will keep each resident safe in their individual apartments?
- Are there railings for safety in common areas and in some of the apartments?
- What measures are in place to prevent falls and slips in the hallways?

- How would the resident alert someone of an emergency?
- Is there help on call 24 hours a day?

Safety is not something that can be taken for granted when it comes to a person with mobility or minor health issues.

In addition, the safety of the facility will also help to assure the resident and their family that they will not be put into harm's way – either intentionally or unintentionally during their stay. A resident should feel just as comfortable in an assisted living facility as they might in their own home.

Staffing Issues

The people who are available for the residents will help not only to ensure the safety and the well-being of the residents, but they can also act as liaisons between the residents and their families.

While the staff cannot be expected to be everywhere at once, the assisted living facility should have a large staff on hand during the daytime hours to help with all of the needs of their residents. The staff should include:

- licensed health care workers (nurses, MAs, etc.)
- regular staff members
- maintenance workers
- management staff

But just having sufficient staff members on hand may not be enough to keep all of the residents and their needs satisfied.

Some questions to ask the assisted living facility include:

- How high or low is the turnover in this facility?
- What are the current licenses and certificates on file for the staff?
- Can I check the validity of these licenses?

- Have background checks been run on all of the staff members?
- Is the staff able to speak clearly and in a language the resident will understand?
- How often are staff members going to check in with the residents?
- What will the staff members do for the residents?
- When will the staff be available to residents?

Health Care Services

When moving into an assisted living facility, it is assumed that residents will not have a large number of problems with which to deal. Yet complications can happen – and health troubles may need to be addressed.

The nurse or other highly skilled staff member will not be on call at all times of the day, but the resident should still have confidence that they will be supported if something happens during their stay at the facility.

Other health care concerns to keep in mind:

- What is the nutritional content of the food served at the facility?
- What health testing options are available?
- How can the facility cater to specific needs for your loved one? i.e. a low cholesterol diet.
- What are the different levels of assistance available at the facility?
- What will happen if the resident requires more supervision or medical care?
- How does the facility support medication checks and refills?
- Are there services to take residents to doctor appointments?
- What conditions is the assisted living facility unable to support? i.e. Alzheimer's.

Activities

Elder residents may not realize how isolated they were when they lived in their own home. The assisted living facility situation can remind them just how nice it is to be around others the same age, enjoying shared activities and games.

Questions to ask about the social aspects of the ALF include:

- What weekly activities are available?
- Are there special outings the residents can enjoy?
- What resources will be available to residents? i.e. library, board games, cards, DVDs, music.
- Is there a regular schedule of activities?
- How are holidays and birthdays celebrated?
- Is there a common area for the residents to share?
- Can all of the residents enjoy the common room at once?
- Are there exercise facilities available?

A resident who is able to interact with others their age tends to be a resident who is not only happier, but also one who stays more mentally fit as the years go on. Having someone to talk to and to share their lives with allows residents to feel less like a patient and more like an everyday person.

Location Concerns

Location can be a concern when the family of the resident is not close by. Having the resident in a city which is easily accessed is something to keep in mind. Conversely, if the family is in one geographic area, it might make more sense to move the parent to this area to make visits easier.

However, the location is not limited to accessibility. Location can also determine the price and the costs associated with the assisted living facility.

Keep in mind that the elderly family member will need to relocate and move into the assisted living facility once the best fit has been chosen. If the senior lives a far distance away, the move can be quite costly, which might also be a factor in the decision making process.

The Comforts of Home?

Though some residents may not feel at home right away, the goal of every assisted living facility should be to have as many of the comforts of home as possible. This includes:

- Separate apartment-like housing
- Clean facilities
- Access to a private kitchen or to the main kitchen
- Access to private shower and bathroom facilities
- Ability to get problems fixed — i.e. if the phone breaks, some-one will come to fix it
- Access to the Internet and phone services

One of the primary concerns of families who want to move a family member into an assisted living facility is the cleanliness of the building — and understandably so. Would-be residents and their families should check to see how often the facilities are cleaned, how they are cleaned, and what happens when the residents need help with cleaning their own housing areas.

Although the cleanliness of the facility may not seem entirely im-portant at first, that "nursing home smell" some facilities have is not something a resident should have to endure.

Moving Out of an Assisted Living Facility

Of course, there may come a time when the elder feels they can handle themselves and a life on their own again — or they may need more care than the assisted living facility is able to offer.

When the health of a resident takes a turn for the worse, a hospital setting or a nursing home facility may become the best option for the physical support of the resident.

In the process of choosing an assisted living facility, the family of the resident will want to check to see what is considered when a resident is unable or unwilling to live at the facility any longer. Are there certain criteria the resident must meet to leave the facility? Are there certain criteria that mean the resident has to leave the facility?

These kinds of questions will allow the family and any care managers involved in the care of the elderly client to better understand what steps will need to be taken should the resident's needs change.

In addition, families should also consider the possibility that the resident may need to move for other reasons. For example, if the facility loses its licensure or Medicaid certification – what steps will be taken then?

An assisted living facility can help to keep an elder as mobile as possible during the later years of their life. And while it might not be the first choice, it is certainly a compromise that can keep everyone happy and healthy.

CHAPTER 13

How to Select a Nursing Home

Unlike assisted living facilities, a nursing home is a place for residents who cannot care for themselves. With extensive resources, residents with medical issues as well as mobility issues can have the support they need when family members are unable to step in to help.

Nursing homes are places where residents can receive more specialized care than they might in more independent living situations. Residents will be able to receive:

- help with bathing
- help with grooming
- help with dressing
- help with moving from one place to another
- specialized therapies – physical therapy, etc.
- skilled nursing services
- access to activities which promote social interaction
- nutritional support for their conditions

- support for more complicated conditions
- constant supervision, if needed
- help when the resident is immobile
- Interaction with staff members and fellow residents
- the transition from ill to well

What many people do not realize about nursing homes is that these facilities are often not the end of health care or used just when residents are facing chronic or terminal diseases. Nursing homes are often a stepping stone to assisted living facilities, especially when a resident is recuperating from a surgery or major illness.

A few months in a nursing home can help a resident become more mobile and thus better able to handle everyday tasks. As a result, they may be able to move into their homes again or into an alternative care situation, as needed.

A Checklist for Choosing the Right Nursing Home

As with any care facility that a resident may be moving into, a number of questions need to be considered before making the final decision as to where to send a resident. Not all nursing homes provide the same services or level of care that a resident may need now or in the future. The following checklist may help you make your final decision:

- What kinds of certifications and/or licenses does the nursing home have?
- What do the state health department records reveal about the cleanliness?
- Are the current residents happy and healthy?
- How many staff members are available to residents?
- What are the qualifications of the staff members?
- Are staff members friendly and helpful?

- What is the standard of care in terms of mental health treatment?
- What range of conditions can the nursing home handle?
- What are the costs of the nursing home? What insurances can cover costs?
- Are the rooms adequate in space? Private? Have windows?
- Is there some privacy for residents?
- What is the condition of the main room?
- Are there activities present for residents to enjoy?
- Are there different levels of activities available for different residents?
- How noisy is the nursing home?
- Are there handrails in place in the halls and bathrooms?
- Is the menu and meal planning overseen by a registered dietician?

As in the selection of the assisted living facility, nursing home selection requires some time from the family members or a geriatric care manager to make sure the facility meets the needs of the resident. Families may want to visit several facilities before making a final decision.

More Tips to Choose the Right Nursing Home

The nursing home chosen may not be the permanent situation for the elderly resident, but that doesn't mean that care shouldn't be taken to ensure that the resident is comfortable and safe at all times.

With some scary stories emerging of elder abuse, families owe it to their loved ones to ensure the nursing home is not only supporting their physical health, but also their mental health.

Check out the staff. It is essential that the nursing home perform thorough background checks on all of the staff members before they are hired. Staff members should also be sent for regular training programs and to update licenses and certifications.

Special services. If the resident is suffering from dementia or Alzheimer's, it is crucial that the resident have access to staff members who are equipped to handle such situations. More often than not the resident who has severe cognitive impairment will require specialized supervision and care.

Loss prevention. Systems should be in place to help residents who might lose their possessions while at the nursing home facility. Are there places where the residents can store valuable items or should those be left with a loved one?

Abuse prevention training. The nursing home facility should also provide abuse prevention training to its staff to ensure residents are treated with the utmost respect and care during their stay in the facility.

Separate units. As some residents may require constant supervision, it may become necessary for the nursing home to have separate wards or units for different types of residents. For residents who may be in the early stages of dementia, for example, the flexibility of having multiple wards available can help to ease a future transition into a more secure unit.

Cultural and religious support. A resident in a nursing home may want to have all of the comforts of home they have already come to enjoy. Having cultural respect and religious service or guidance available can help to keep a resident at ease during their stay.

Care plan updates. Checking to see how often care plans for residents are updated will give families the chance to see how a resident is progressing and whether they need more or less specialized care.

Privacy issues. Residents may want to have their own space from time to time to feel as though they are in a place which is more like home.

Having access to a phone line that is out of the way of others as well as to have a place to sit and reflect without interruption can be helpful to residents.

In addition, if family members want to visit, a private area where the resident and the family members can interact is much appreciated.

In the visits to various nursing homes, families of residents will want to eat the food, go to the rooms, and see the home from the point of view of their loved one. After all, if the family member wouldn't stay in the nursing home, why should the resident be happy about the choice?

Communication for Out of Town Family Members

As many families are now spread out around the globe, it may become necessary for the elderly resident to be in a nursing home which is far away from their hometown or from the cities where their relatives reside.

In these common situations, it is advised that residents and their families know that the lines of communication are always open and available.

The resident should be able to call on a regular basis and receive calls as they come in from their children or other loved ones. The staff should also be frequently updating the families on the condition of the resident or be readily available to answer questions via phone, email, or fax, if possible.

Since the loved ones of the resident may not be able to visit regularly, this open communication will allow everyone to be assured of the condition of the resident and of their health and stability in the nursing home.

CHAPTER 14

Psychological Aspects of Aging

Aging is a process which takes place from the time a person is born until the time they die. Though the human body grows for many years, inevitably, it will begin to break down and cause trouble.

But while the body provides clear symptoms and changes which the eye can see and observe, the mind can be trickier when it comes to aging. Though the mind can continue to be as sharp as ever as a person ages, there are specific problems which elderly people experience more often than their younger counterparts.

The Mind and Aging

As the body ages, the mind too begins to age. The brain and its neural network begin to decline, causing memories to fade and mental acuity to lessen. These changes to the mind have become stereotypical reminders of the process of aging, but they are not the end of mental dysfunction as the years pass.

The mental fitness of an aging person changes with each passing year. Remember that as a person ages, their friends and family members also age, causing their social network to shrink and their connections to lessen. In addition, the aging of a person is also a reminder that their youth has been lost. With retirement comes a particular loss of purpose in many elderly people. They are unsure of their identity outside of their working life, becoming confused as to what their purpose in life may be now.

Aging can be a scary time in which a person does not know what might happen next, what their symptoms mean, and how becoming older might affect their everyday lives and plans. Older people can experience:

- clinical depression
- anxiety
- memory loss
- anger issues
- disengagement in life

Clinical depression is a considerable concern among those who may be considered elderly. The loss of purpose in life can lead to periods of sadness, which can even lead to troubles with suicidal thoughts. More often, however, depression can show up as hostility and anger in an elderly person. Families who notice large changes in mood should be aware that depression might be the cause, rather than just anger.

Treating depression can be accomplished with the help of antidepressant medications, as prescribed by a doctor, as well as by therapy appointments with a licensed therapist or counselor. Many times, people who increase their social network will also have an easier time lifting themselves from depression.

Anxiety can be a common occurrence among the elderly. Seniors may be concerned for their own health as well as for the health of those who take care of them. In addition, some elderly people fear they will become a burden to others, thus increasing their anxiety even more. Anxiety can also be treated with prescription medications and with therapy.

Memory loss can often be caused simply by not exercising the brain as often as one might have in the past. Since the memory works like a muscle, the brain must be 'exercised' as often as possible. By participating in regular games and learning activities, an older person can easily maintain their memory and even improve it.

The brain may age along with the body, but new neural networks can be created when an elderly person takes the time to engage themselves. In fact, disengagement from the rest of the world and social networks can decrease memory function. By taking the time to be with other elderly people, a person can begin to boost their mental acuity and begin to feel more like a productive part of life.

Other possible treatments for mood changes and for other mental disorders can be discussed with a primary care doctor or a gerontologist who specializes in the care of elderly people. In addition, if mental problems persist, an appointment with a neurologist may be warranted to help rule out any physical disorders that may be affecting the mental health of a person.

Other Tips to Slow the Aging of the Mind

The body is a miraculous piece of "machinery." It not only heals itself in many cases, but it can also repair itself as the body begins to age, slowing down the deterioration of the brain and all of its functions.

Here are a few ways in which an elderly person can help to prevent the psychological impact of aging:

- maintain friendships
- talk with family members often
- eat a low fat, low sodium diet
- drink alcohol in moderation
- exercise regularly

- quit smoking
- have a positive attitude about life and its challenges
- make plans for the future
- have coping mechanisms for stress

Taking care of one's health directly affects the way the brain will function, both now and in the future. A person who can begin to take care of their health now will find that their mind is sharper and they feel more engaged with their life.

Aging is a time when many things change in one's life, but that doesn't mean that a person needs to feel miserable. In fact, many elderly people report that they enjoy their senior years more than their younger years.

CHAPTER 15

The Unlicensed Practice
of Law in Florida

Non-lawyers can get into serious legal hot water if they attempt to pass themselves off as lawyers. The reasons are self-evident. But how do you define the so-called Unlicensed Practice of Law (UPL)? Why do people engage in this practice? What punishments might they incur?

In Florida, UPL is defined through case law as opposed to through some universal, unchanging definition. In other words, context matters.

More specifically, the law says:

> The practice of law . . . includes the giving of legal advice and counsel to others as to their rights and obligations under the law and in preparation of legal instruments, including contracts, by which legal rights are either obtained, secured, or given away. . . .[42]

The biggest concern that the court has in defining, preventing, and regulating legal practice is "the protection of the public from incompetent, unethical, or irresponsible representation."[43]

To determine whether a non-attorney's actions constituted UPL, you must examine existing case law and view the non-lawyer's actions (or non actions) in the context of these other cases.

Examples of Courts Ruling That a Non-Attorney Is Engaged in Unlicensed Practice of Law:

- When someone gives advice, consults, explains, or recommends legal documents, that constitutes UPL.[44]
- The Supreme Court, in a 1992 Advisory Opinion, said that a non-lawyer who assembles, drafts, executes or funds a living trust for a third party is engaging in UPL.[45]
- A non-attorney who obtains a standard legal form – something you might print off a reputable internet site, for instance – and then engages in any "creative" drafting may be charged with the Unlicensed Practice of Law if he or she does anything more than act as a secretary or scrivener.[46]
- The court holds that amateurs practicing law are as potentially harmful to Florida communities as are amateurs who practice surgery.[47]
- In Florida, practicing law without a license is a third degree felony – a very serious crime that can lead to lengthy jail sentences.[48]

UPL and Medicaid Planning: Why There Has Been a "Vast Proliferation" of Non-Attorneys Advising the Public

In recent years, there has been a great increase in the number of non-attorneys who have begun to provide Medicaid planning services. In many instances, the services being provided by non–attorney Medicaid planners appear to be very similar to the services being provided by attorneys who provide Medicaid planning services.

As mentioned in Chapter 6, the Federal Deficit Reduction Act of 2005 (DRA) was enacted into law in Florida on November 1, 2007. The Deficit Reduction Act made significant changes to *Medicaid Qualifying Annuities*. One of the major changes made by the DRA was that balloon style Medicaid Qualifying Annuities could no longer be used to shelter assets for unmarried Medicaid applicants. Without question, the most commonly used insurance/annuity product used to obtain Medicaid benefits for unmarried Medicaid applicants in Florida prior to November 1, 2007 was the balloon style Medicaid Qualifying Annuity.

Although the balloon style Medicaid Qualifying Annuity could still be used by the community spouse after the DRA, the new law also now requires that the State of Florida be named the first beneficiary on a Medicaid Qualifying Annuity used by a community spouse to shelter assets to obtain Medicaid benefits for his or her spouse. For all of these reasons, Medicaid Qualifying Annuities went from being one of the most commonly used Medicaid planning strategies in Florida to a strategy that now is rarely used in Florida.

Prior to November 1, 2007, it appeared that the vast majority of non-attorney Medicaid planners involved in Medicaid planning were Florida-licensed insurance agents, who limited their Medicaid planning services to the sale of Medicaid Qualifying Annuities. Prior to November 1, 2007, most non-attorney Medicaid planners were neither involved in counseling prospective Medicaid applicants on the laws to obtain Medicaid benefits nor the preparation and submission of the Medicaid files to the Florida Department of Children and Families (DCF).

Because of the changes in Florida rules regarding Medicaid Qualifying Annuities after November 1, 2007, financial planners who made most of their income from commissions from the sale of Medicaid Qualifying Annuities effectively no longer had a source of income. Because of this legal change, many of those same financial planners, who previously were involved exclusively in the sale of Medicaid Qualifying Annuities, prior to November 1, 2007, have now become *Medicaid Planners* and are counseling the public on the Florida laws to obtain Medicaid benefits. Since November 1, 2007, there has been a vast proliferation in the number non-attorney Medicaid planners who are advising the public on how to obtain Medicaid benefits. Some of those individuals are insurance agents, and some of those individuals have no state license of any kind. There have even been reports of individuals who have lost their insurance license from the state of Florida, and they are now providing Medicaid planning services to the public. There has even been a report of a disbarred attorney who has established a Medicaid planning company.

An Example to Highlight the Hidden Dangers: A Life's Savings, Wiped Out in Months

Consider this nightmare scenario:

Your great Aunt Eloise, who is a resident of Pasco County, Florida, is hospitalized with complications from her diabetes. The medical crisis disables her, and she needs to be placed in a nursing home as a permanent resident.

To "help" Aunt Eloise now that she is sick, you ask a friend or family member — a non-attorney — to draft a document for her called a Durable Power of Attorney (DPOA). This document is intended to serve as a blueprint for your aunt's legal and financial planning.

Two years pass, and your great aunt suffers a stroke. Now, she can no longer make her own decisions. So you go to your attorney to ask him to assist Aunt Eloise with applying for Medicaid to defray her nursing home care costs. In Florida, these costs can amount to $6,000 a month or more, depending on the facility and care needed.

But your attorney has some terrible news: the Durable Power of Attorney documents that the non-lawyer drew up do not contain provisions needed to proceed with Medicaid planning.

More simply put: Aunt Eloise will not be getting the $6,000 per month she needs to pay for her care. What happens next? Who will pay for her care? Will Aunt Eloise's life savings be drained away, perhaps in months, due to a momentarily lapse of reason and improper planning?

The scenario above is just a single instance of the kind of tragedy that can unfold when unqualified people participate in the Unlicensed Practice of Law (UPL).

The moral is: you need to choose your representation carefully!

How to Make the Safest Choices

There are legal and ethical considerations that need to be made when choosing a professional to help you with restructuring the assets and income of your loved one to obtain Medicaid benefits. To be eligible to practice law in Florida, an individual must be a member in good standing with the Florida Bar. If a person who provides Medicaid planning services is not a member of the Florida Bar, and you are considering the use of such a person to obtain Medicaid benefits for your loved one, the following considerations need to be made:

- By definition, a non-attorney has no license to practice law in Florida. The person is unlicensed to practice law.
- Because the person is not licensed by the Florida Bar, the person is therefore not regulated by the Florida Bar. This means that a non-attorney is not required to follow the rules and procedures that attorneys must follow to maintain their law license with the Florida Bar. If you are injured by a non-attorney who is providing Medicaid planning services, what entity is going to make you whole and discipline the non-attorney if they are not regulated by the Florida Bar? Attorneys who practice law in every state are regulated by

numerous rules and regulations governing their conduct. The primary reason for these rules and regulations is to protect the public from being harmed by people who are not qualified to practice law.

Example: Carmela holds valid durable power of attorney for her father Xavier, who is a resident of Santa Rosa County, Florida.

Xavier is a long-term resident of a skilled nursing facility. Xavier's gross monthly income is $2,050 per month, which is slightly below the 2012 Florida income cap of $2,094 per month.

Instead of hiring an attorney, Carmela hires a very likable and popular insurance salesman named Tony, who is holding himself out as a Medicaid Planning Specialist.

Tony was recommended by the nursing facility to Carmela. Tony was paying the nursing home representative $200 for each client referral he received from the facility. Tony also holds a real estate license, and he is actively involved in real estate sales.

Tony, the non-attorney Medicaid planner, is somewhat familiar with Florida Medicaid rules, and he recommends that Carmella purchase income-producing property to restructure Xavier's assets and bring Xavier below the $2,000 asset limit

Upon hiring Tony, Xavier had $200,000 in his checking account.

Tony charged a fee of $6,000 for his advice to restructure the assets. Because Tony was also a real estate agent, Tony recommended that Carmela purchase a piece of rented real estate on which he was the listing agent. Tony then sold the real estate to Xavier (for $192,000 minus his commission), and Tony earned a commission on the sale of the real estate. The property was rented for $300 per month. In the consulting agreement, Tony wrote into the contract with Carmela that if the rental property now owned by Xavier were ever sold at any point in the future, Tony would be entitled to 50% of the gross profit on the sale of the property. Tony then submitted the Medicaid application to the Florida Department of Children and Families (DCF), and the Medicaid application was denied.

The Medicaid application was denied for two reasons:

1. Tony failed to advise Carmela that the $300 monthly rent put Xavier over the $2,094 income cap, and no qualified income trust was established.

2. The DCF caseworker determined that the $300 per month rent was not a *fair market value rent*, and the rental property was determined by DCF to be a countable asset because the rent was not a fair market value rent.

    In addition to failing to properly advise Carmela on all the legal ramifications of his advice, Tony, if he were an attorney, may have also committed some serious ethical violations. First of all, since he was the real estate agent in the sale, and he earned a commission on the sale of the rental property, that action raised a serious question about a conflict of interest. Second, by sharing in the profit on the sale of Xavier's rental property, Tony also acted in a way that would raise serious questions about a conflict of interest. Further, by failing to advise Carmela on the legal ramifications of all of the consequences regarding the purchase of the rental property, Tony failed to adequately represent Carmela and Xavier, and the Medicaid application failed. Since Tony is not licensed or regulated by the Florida Bar, what Florida government agency would be responsible for regulating Tony's conduct and protecting Carmela and Xavier from the harm that Tony caused them?

A third problem with hiring a non-attorney Medicaid planner to perform Medicaid planning services is that non-attorneys, since by definition they are not attorneys, could not be covered by legal malpractice insurance.

Example: Consider the preceding example regarding Carmela, Xavier and Tony.

After the problems Tony caused Xavier and Carmela because Tony was not licensed, regulated, or trained as a Florida attorney, the family had to locate an experienced Elder Law attorney to fix the damage caused by Tony. By the time the new elder law attorney was hired, the Qualified Income Trust was established, and the rental property was rented out for a fair market value rent. Eight months had passed since Tony first told Carmela he would obtain Medicaid benefits for Xavier. The facility had a private pay rate of $220 per day during that time. Therefore, the base cost to Xavier was $6,600 per month. In addition, other incidentals (such as over-the-counter medications, laundry, transportation to and from doctors and hospitals, etc.), which are covered by Medicaid, cost Xavier an additional $600 per month. Accordingly, Xavier now owed the nursing home $57,600 ($7,200 x 8 months) for the cost of his care for the past 8 months.

Carmela sued Tony for the $57,600 owed to the facility, but she quickly found out that Tony had no legal malpractice insurance because he was not an attorney. Carmela then discovered there were multiple other lawsuits pending against Tony because of failed Medicaid cases and that Tony had just filed bankruptcy to protect himself against the pending lawsuits. Unfortunately, after learning of these circumstances, Carmela realized that Tony would not be able to make Carmela or her father whole.

To add to Carmela's woes, the nursing facility had asked Carmela to sign the admissions documents to the nursing home, when her father was admitted to the facility. Carmela was under a lot of stress. She did not understand it at the time, but one of the admissions documents she signed made her personally liable for any unpaid bill at the nursing home, and now Carmella owed $57,600 to the nursing home.

The actions of Tony in the preceding examples can also lead to potential liability for the nursing home and its employees.

Example: Consider the preceding two examples regarding Carmela, Xavier and Tony.

After realizing that she was personally liable for the $57,600 owed to the facility, Carmela contacted another attorney who concentrated his practice in negligent referral lawsuits. After listening to the fact pattern, the attorney advised Carmela to sue the nursing home under a theory of negligent referral.

A lawsuit was filed against the nursing home, and the facility decided to settle the case out of court, because the corporate owners realized that the nursing home employee was clearly negligent in referring Carmela to Tony, who was not qualified to handle the Medicaid case.

The nursing home also fired the employee, because she negligently referred Carmela to Tony, and because she accepted $200 payment from Tony as a kickback.

The Florida Bar Standing Committee for Unlicensed Practice of Law has also recently addressed the issue of non-attorneys providing Medicaid planning services. In a letter dated May 13, 2009, the Committee issued the following statement in their letter:

The committee voted that based on existing case law, the following activities would constitute the unlicensed practice of law: establishing irrevocable trusts, establishing Qualified Income Trusts, and hiring an attorney to review, prepare or modify documents for customers if payment to the attorney was through the company. [49]

The Florida Bar Standing Committee voted that the following activities would have to be determined on a case-by-case basis: restructuring assets, counseling customers on the best way to get Medicaid approval, and advertising as an "elder counselor".[50]

Example: Alejandra contacted a non-attorney Medicaid planner Steve, who is a Florida licensed insurance agent and holds himself out as a "Medicaid Planning Specialist."

Alejandra's father, Armando, has been a resident at an assisted living facility in Escambia County, Florida. The owner of the assisted living facility referred Alejandra to Steve.

The assisted living facility can no longer meet Armando's medical needs, and Armando must now move to a skilled nursing facility.

Armando's gross monthly income is $4,000 per month, which includes his Social Security and a DFAS pension, from Armando's prior military service in the United States Air Force. The $4,000 per month in income had been just enough to pay the $3,800 per month bill at the assisted living facility.

The private pay bill at the new nursing home is going to be $7,100 per month, and Armando has no money saved up. He generally only has about $1,500 left over in his checking account each month after paying the assisted living bill.

The insurance agent Steve tells Alejandra that he has drafted durable powers of attorney and Qualified Income Trusts for his clients in the past, and that he has successfully obtained Medicaid benefits for nursing home residents in the past. Steve advised Alejandra that Armando will need a Qualified Income Trust to obtain Medicaid benefits, because Armando's monthly income exceeds the $2,094 income cap. Steve quotes a fee of $3,800 to draft a durable power of attorney, a Qualified Income Trust, and submit the Medicaid application for Armando.

Steve is also a Notary Public. Steve prepares the durable power of attorney for Armando, and he goes to the nursing home to visit with Armando and execute the durable power of attorney.

Steve properly executes the power of attorney with two witnesses and then sets up an appointment with Alejandra, who Armando has named as his attorney-in-fact in his newly signed durable power of attorney. Steve then prepares a Qualified Income Trust and has Alejandra sign it the presence of two witnesses. Steve tells Alejandra that he has provided these exact same services for many Medicaid applicants in the past, and all of his cases have been approved.

After Armando's Medicaid is submitted to DCF, the Medicaid application is denied. Unfortunately, Steve was not aware that Florida adopted a new power of attorney statute on October 1, 2011. Steve continued to use the same power of attorney document after October 1, 2011 that he had been providing to clients for the past few years.

Under the new power of attorney statute, a "general grant of authority" is no longer effective, and to establish an irrevocable trust, a separate provision in the durable power document authorizing the establishment of the trust needed to be initialed or signed by Armando. Steve was not aware of the new power attorney statute, so Steve continued to use the same durable power of attorney document he had always used in the past.

By the time the decision was issued by the DCF caseworker in Armando's Medicaid case, three months had passed, and the unpaid bill in the nursing home exceeded $21,000. Neither Armando nor Alejandra had sufficient funds available to pay for the unpaid private pay bill in the nursing home, and when the Medicaid case was denied, the nursing facility issued a discharge notice to Armando, due to his failure to pay the bill.

Personal Service Contracts are also a very popular Medicaid planning strategy that are used by unmarried Medicaid applicants to obtain Medicaid benefits. However, caution must be exercised when using personal service contracts.

Example: Francisco is a resident of Indian River County, Florida, and he is a long-term resident in a nursing home.

His daughter Marisol is his attorney-in-fact under a properly executed durable power of attorney prepared by a Florida licensed attorney. Francisco currently has $800,000 in savings, but the nursing facility is charging $7,500 per month, and Francisco is expected to live another twenty years.

Francisco was recently diagnosed with dementia, and he is not expected to ever leave the nursing home. The business office at the nursing home refers residents' families to a non-attorney Medicaid Planner named Goldey, who is also an insurance agent.

Marisol meets with Goldey, and Goldey states that she has prepared personal service contracts for Medicaid applicants in the past, and all of her cases have been approved.

Goldey suggests that Marisol consider transferring approximately $800,000 to herself, under a personal service contract, to reduce Francisco's countable assets below $2,000. Goldey states that since Marisol is the only child of Francisco, and Marisol is the sole beneficiary of Francisco's Will, it would make perfect sense to transfer the money to Marisol. Marisol agrees, Goldey prepares the personal service contract, and Marisol issues a check to herself for $790,000.

Goldey charged a $9,000 fee to prepare the personal service contract. Goldey was not familiar with the IRS rules regarding personal service contracts, and Goldey never mentioned anything to Marisol about income taxes.

Goldey submitted the Medicaid application with the $790,000

personal services contract. DCF promptly denied the Medicaid case, based on the fact the $790,000 payment was not a fair market value payment for Marisol's services.

Marisol really liked Goldey, so Marisol just decided to forget about the whole thing and use the $790,000 to pay the private pay bill at the nursing home.

The following year, the IRS audited Marisol due to a separate sole proprietorship business she owned. During the IRS audit, the IRS discovered the $790,000 payment and the personal service contract. Marisol ended up having to pay the United States Treasury $270,000 in back income taxes, interest and penalties.

Protecting the Public

What should you do if you have been injured by the unlicensed practice of law – or become aware of the unlicensed practice of law?

The Florida Bar's approach to investigating allegations of the unlicensed practice of law has been described as *complaint driven*. In other words, there is no way for the Florida Bar to become aware of alleged unlicensed practice of law activity unless someone reports the activity to the Florida Bar.

Another way to look at the unlicensed practice of law in Florida is that it is very unlikely that a particular instance of UPL will be investigated by the Florida Bar, unless someone reports the alleged UPL activity to the Florida Bar. As a practical matter, the way for the public to be protected is for members of the public to report alleged UPL activities to the Florida Bar. Remember the famous words of Edmund Burke: "All that is necessary for the triumph of evil is that good men do nothing."

If you become aware of, or have been injured by any of the following activities, you should report them to the Florida Bar:

- The drafting of qualified income trust documents by a non-attorney.
- The drafting of a personal service contract by a non-attorney.
- The drafting of a durable power of attorney by a non-attorney.
- The drafting of a living trust, an irrevocable trust, a Will, a living will, or a health care surrogate by a non-attorney.
- A person who is not licensed as an attorney and who states he/she is an attorney.
- A person not licensed as an attorney who appears to be giving legal advice to members of the public.
- Any person who has been paid a "kick back" by a nursing home or assisted living employee in return for a client referral.

The Florida Bar provides a short form that can be quickly completed to report alleged instances of UPL. To obtain the form from the Florida Bar you can call them toll free at 1-800-235-8619, or log on to their website at www.FloridaBar.org.

Remember, if you take no action against alleged instances of UPL, there is no way the Florida Bar can become aware of the problem or do anything to correct the problem.

Key Points to Remember Regarding Durable Power of Attorney and UPL:

Whether the senior lives in a nursing facility, or some other environment, one of his or her most pressing issues almost certainly involves how to finance the cost of their care. As discussed earlier, this care can cost upwards of $6,000 a month. If a resident stays in a nursing home for five years, those costs can exceed $350,000.

To qualify for Medicaid, a senior often needs to engage in rather sophisticated planning; thus, the Durable Power of Attorney document must be carefully constructed.

If a non-lawyer engages in the UPL and drafts a DPOA or other document related to estate planning, the senior may experience dramatic legal problems, including – potentially – disqualification from Medicaid.

The Durable Power of Attorney gives a third party, often known as an agent, authority and power to make decisions and act on someone's behalf. The agent will often be able to enter into contracts and create trusts on behalf of the senior as well as to design and execute a Medicaid plan.

Standard DPOA documents – so-called fill in the blank documents – *may be inadequate to sufficiently protect the senior.* It is generally far better practice for the resident to turn to an experienced Florida elder care attorney to draw up a customized DPOA.

Protecting Legal Rights

What can you do to protect yourself and the senior you care about?

Protecting Your Own Legal Rights

- Refrain from drafting a DPOA document for any senior or any other family members;
- Refrain from drafting or executing any other legal document, such as an estate plan document;
- Refrain from advising the senior about what forms to get, how to fill them out, etc.
- Refer the senior to a Florida elder law attorney, who can help the senior structure her income and assets, develop effective options, and ensure an ethical and positive outcome.

Protecting the Senior

- *If the senior is of sound mind and body* – he or she should consider connecting with a Florida elder care and estate planning attorney to discuss documents and mechanisms to protect his or her assets and ensure effective end-of-life care.

• *If the senior is no longer able to make decisions effectively* — again, a visit to a qualified estate planning and elder care attorney may be appropriate.

Preparation is the best defense against costly misjudgments. Often, seniors and/or concerned family members engage in dubious practices, like the Unlicensed Practice of Law, because they find themselves blind sided by unexpected problems. Panicked, they rush to solve these issues and unwittingly create potentially catastrophic legal and financial problems.

Fixing Problems that Have Already Happened

If you or another non-lawyer has already drafted a legal document or engaged in other practices that you may believe might have constituted UPL under Florida Law, you can take action to rectify the situation before it becomes problematic and/or leads to penalties, or other legal problems. The sooner and more proactively you address any problems — even problems that may seem insurmountable right now — the better the likelihood that you will receive the compassionate, attentive help that you need to make it through your crisis. You should contact an experienced elder care attorney right away to discuss your legal questions in a confidential setting.

Florida Medicaid Managed Care Update

In May 2011 the Florida Legislature voted to adopt managed care for the Florida Medicaid program. This means that the entire Florida Medicaid program will at some point be turned over to privately managed Medicaid healthcare providers. Florida lawmakers see this as a way to put financial limits on the Florida Medicaid budget. For Florida to adopt a privately managed Medicaid program, the new Florida law must be approved by the federal government. As of the publication date of the second edition of this book, the federal government has not yet granted approval for the new Florida law. If the federal government authorizes managed care for Florida Medicaid, this will be a very substantial change in the way the Florida Medicaid programs are currently administered.

To learn when the change takes place and what they involve, regularly visit:

www.EstateLegalPlanning.com

Chapter 2

1. *Florida Economic Self-Sufficiency Public Assistance Policy Manual* (*"Policy Manual"*), Section 1640.0543.02.

2. *Policy Manual*, Section 1640.0537.

3. *Policy Manual*, Sections 1640.0544, 1640.0548, 1840.0501, and 1840.0504.

4. 42 U.S.C. Sec 1396p(d)(4)(A), 42 U.S.C. Sec 1369 p(d)(4)(B), and 42 U.S.C. Sec 1396 p(d)(4)(C) are of particular importance.

5. The "Miller Trust" title stems from a case called *Miller v. Ibarra*, 746 F. Supp. 19 (D. Colo. 1990). 42 U.S.C. Sec 1396 (d)(4)(B) effectively codifies the requirements of the *Miller v. Ibarra* case.

6. Florida Statutes, Chapter 709, contains the statutory rules regarding Florida durable power of attorney.

Chapter 4

7. *Thomas v. Florida Department of Children and Families*, 707 So. 2d 954 (Fla. 4th DCA 1998).

8. *Florida Economic Self-Sufficiency Public Assistance Policy Manual*, Appendix A-14.

9. Section 61 of the Internal Revenue Code.

10. The specific provision of OBRA '93 that authorizes the Pooled Trust is 42 U.S.C. Section 1396 (p)(d)(4)(C). For this reason, Pooled Trusts are often referred to as (d)(4)(C) trusts.

11. Section 1640.0576.80. OBRA '93 is also known for other important trusts: 1.) The Qualified Income Trust is authorized under 42 U.S.C. Section 1396 (p)(d)(4)(B) of OBRA '93. 2.) 42 U.S.C. 1396 (p)(d)(4)(C) of OBRA '93 authorizes a disability trust for individuals under the age of 65, and the trust *cannot* be created by the disabled individual.

12. Three primary provisions of the *Policy Manual* make this clear (Sections 1640.0501, 1640.0548 and 1840.0501).

13. *Policy Manual*, Section 1840.0504.

14. Social Security Act, Sections 1917(d)(3)(A) and 1917(e)(5).

15. Internal Revenue Code, Section 2503. The divestment penalty divisor is completely different from the federal $12,000 annual gift tax exclusion, under Internal Revenue Code Section 2503(b). This provision of the Internal Revenue Code states that a person can gift up to $12,000 per year, without having to file a gift tax return (IRS form 709).

Chapter 5

16. *Florida Economic Self-Sufficiency Public Assistance Policy Manual* outlines the authorization of spousal refusal under Florida law at *Policy Manual*, Section 1640.0314.03.

17. *Connor v. Southwest Florida Regional Medical Center, Inc.*, 668 So. 2d 175 (Fla. 1996).

Chapter 6

18. F.A.C. 65A-1.712, SSI-Related Medicaid Resource Eligibility Criteria.

19. F.A.C. Section 65A-1.712 has five primary sections: 65A-1.712(1) through 65A-1.712(5). Section 65A-1.712(1) "Resource Limits" and Section 65A-1.712(2) "Exclusions" contain a few changes related to the Deficit Reduction Act. Section 65A.1.712(3) "Transfers of Resources and Income" contains the most significant changes to Florida law. Section 65A-1.712(4) "Spousal Impoverishment" contains provisions related to circumstances which might affect the community spouse. Section 65A-1.712(5) "Other Resource Policies" contains the details regarding restrictions on a Medicaid applicant's home equity and entrance fees for Continuing Care Retirement Communities.

20. F.A.C. Section 65A-1.712(2)(g) contains a discussion of changes related to long-term care insurance.

21. F.A.C. Section 65A-1.712(3), "Transfers of Resources and Income", contains a number of significant provisions.

22. F.A.C. Section 65A-1.712(3)(a) & (b) address changes related to annuities. Section 65A-1.712(b)(1) requires that Medicaid applicants and their spouses must disclose any annuities that they own.

23. F.A.C. Section 65A-1.712(b)(3) addresses individual retirement accounts (IRA's).

24. F.A.C., Section 65A-1.712(3)(d)(1) and Section 65A-1.712(5)(d)(4)(e).

25. F.A.C., Section 65A-1.712(3)(d)(3).

26. F.A.C., Section 65A-1.172(3)(d)(3).

27. F.A.C., Section 65A-1.712(3)(9)(d)(4) addresses the new Florida treatment of life estates.

28. F.A.C., Section 65A-1.712(3)(d)(4)(g) contains the new provisions regarding the calculation of penalty periods for gifts.

29. F.A.C., F.A.C., Section 65A-1.712(4) deals with spousal impoverishment provisions.

30. F.A.C., Section 65A-1.712(4)(f).

31. F.A.C., Section 65A-1.712(5)(9) addresses new limitation on home equity. The Deficit Reduction Act allowed states to choose a limit of $750,000 or $500,000 in home equity. Florida selected a limit of $500,000.

32. F.A.C., Section 65A-1, 712(5)(b).

Chapter 7

33. Florida Statutes, Chapter 709, contains the statutory rules regarding Florida durable powers of attorney.

34. Florida Statutes, Chapter 709.08.

35. The Florida probate code is set forth in chapters 731 through 739 of the Florida Statutes.

36. Florida Statute 733.701 requires that notice be given to creditors. Furthermore, Florida Statute 733.2121(3)(d) requires probate estates, of any deceased individual over the age of 55, in the state of Florida, to serve notice to the Agency for Health Care Administration.

37. Article X, Section 4 of the Florida State Constitution provides protection of the homestead against most creditors.

38. The *Policy Manual* addresses this issue in section 1640.0505.04.

39. See *Policy Manual,* Section 1640.0505.04.

40. See *Policy Manual,* Section 1640.0505.04.

41. The applicable provisions of the *Policy Manual*, Sections are 1640.0305.03, 1640.0551, 1640.0614.03, and Policy Manual Appendix A-17.

Chapter 15

42. Florida State ex rel. The Florida Bar v. Sperry, 140 Sd.2d 587, 591 (Fla. 1962).

190 NOTES

43. The Florida Bar v. Moses, 380, 380 So.2d 412, 417 (Fla. 1980).

44. Floridabar.org, "Unlicensed Practice of Law", sourced March 2, 2012.

45. The Florida Bar RE: Advisory Opinion – Nonlawyer Preparation of Living Trusts, 613 So.2d 426; December 24, 1992.

46. State v. Buyers Service Co., 292 s.c. 426, 430, 357, S.E.2d 15, 17 (1987).

47. In re Baker, 8 N.J. 321, 85A.2d 505, 514 (1951).

48. Chapter 10 of the rules regulating the Florida Bar.

49. Public Letter issued by the Florida Bar Standing Committee for Unlicensed Practice of Law, dated May 13, 2009.

50. Public Letter issued by the Florida Bar Standing Committee for Unlicensed Practice of Law, dated May 13, 2009.

GLOSSARY

Activities of Daily Living (ADLs) – The things a person normally does in daily living, including any daily activity one performs for self-care (such as feeding, bathing, dressing, grooming), work, homemaking, and leisure. The ability or inability to perform ADLs can be used as a very practical measure of ability/disability in many disorders.

Agency for Health Care Administration (AHCA) – A Florida government agency involved in the licensing of health care facilities and health care providers. AHCA is also involved in the disbursement of funds to health care providers and the recovery of Medicaid benefits that have been erroneously paid out.

assisted living facility (ALF) – A place of residence for individuals who can no longer live independently but do not yet need nursing home care. To be classified as an assisted living facility, it must have a license issued by the state of Florida. Some assisted living facilities accept the Medicaid Waiver program and other ALFs accept the Medicaid Diversion Program. Some ALFs accept both Medicaid programs, and some ALFs accept no Medicaid programs at all.

attorney-in-fact – A person named in a written power of attorney document to act on behalf of the person who signs the document, called the principal. An attorney-in-fact is an agent of the principal. The attorney-in-fact's power and responsibilities depend on the specific powers granted in the power of attorney document.

benefit recovery – Under some circumstances, the state may seek the recovery (repayment) of Medicaid benefits paid out. If a Medicaid recipient dies, the state will attempt to recover from any nonexempt assets in the probate estate. The state will also seek the recovery of any Medicaid benefits paid if they were obtained though fraud.

burial savings account – A burial savings account is a bank savings account that has been designated to pay for burial expenses. The *Florida Economic Self-Sufficiency Public Assistance Policy Manual ("Policy Manual")* provides that up to $2,500 can be set aside in a savings account if the funds are clearly designated for burial. The account is an exempt asset.

CARES – An acronym for a department within the Florida Department of Elder Affairs. CARES stands for "Comprehensive Assessment and Review for Long-Term Care Services." Upon application for Medicaid benefits, the Medicaid applicant will be evaluated by a caseworker from the CARES team to establish the medical need for nursing home or assisted living care.

COLA – This is an acronym for "Cost of Living Adjustment." Each year, sources of income, such as SSI or social security retirement, are adjusted to keep pace with price levels in the general economy.

community spouse (CS) – The spouse who remains in the community when the institutionalized spouse (or IS) applies for Medicaid benefits in a nursing home or an assisted living facility.

community spouse resource allowance (CSRA) – This is the maximum dollar amount of countable assets the community spouse is allowed to have for Medicaid qualifications. The 2012 CSRA is $113,640.

Data Exchange – Data shared by the state of Florida and the federal government regarding Medicaid applicants. Used to help verify the Medicaid applicant's eligibility for Medicaid.

Deficit Reduction Act of 2005 (DRA) – Federal legislation signed by President Bush on February 8, 2006, and considered to be a controversial law by many elder law practitioners. The law has several harsh rules that are part of an effort to make it more difficult for individuals to obtain Medicaid benefits.

demographic information – Basic information about an individual, such as age, sex, race and national origin, that is used to identify the person.

designated representative – The person selected by the Medicaid applicant (or the Medicaid applicant's legal representative) to make his or her application for Medicaid benefits. There are no particular requirements to be a designated representative.

diversion (income allocation) – The amount of income that can be diverted to the community spouse each month from the Medicaid recipient's income. The amount of income allocated to the community spouse can be increased, based on the total shelter expenses of the community spouse.

divestment penalty division (penalty divisor) – The dollar figure that is supposed to represent the average monthly cost of a private skilled nursing facility in the state of Florida. The current divestment penalty divisor is $5,000. The penalty divisor is also used to calculate Medicaid penalty periods for gifts.

durable power of attorney – A legal document that authorizes a person to make financial decisions on behalf of another person. The Florida power of attorney statute requires a durable power of attorney to be executed with the same formalities as a real estate deed. A durable power of attorney remains in effect if the person who creates the document — called the principal — becomes incapacitated. If a power of attorney is not specifically made "durable", it automatically expires if the principal becomes incapacitated.

enhanced life estate deed (Lady Bird deed) – A Lady Bird deed is a special life estate deed that is used in Medicaid planning to avoid both probate and the disqualification period created by the standard life estate deed. Unlike the traditional life estate deed, the Lady Bird deed allows the grantor (the holder of the life estate) to retain complete control of the property without the consent of the remainder interest holder. Since the grantor retains full power over the property to sell or otherwise do anything with the property, without consent of the remainder interest holder, a Lady Bird deed does not constitute a transfer or gift for Medicaid purposes.

ex parte – Latin for "on or from one side." If an individual transferred from one Medicaid program to another, the application for the new Medicaid program would be classified as "ex parte." For example, some people improve and can transfer from a nursing home to an assisted living facility. The Medicaid application for benefits in the assisted living facility would be referred to as an "ex parte" Medicaid application.

fair hearing – This is an administrative proceeding that a person has a right to pursue, if the Medicaid application is denied or if the Medicaid applicant is otherwise dissatisfied with the outcome of the Medicaid application.

Florida Department of Children and Families (DCF) – The Florida government agency that is responsible for processing the financial applications for Medicaid, Food Stamps and several other Florida government entitlement programs.

Florida Department of Elder Affairs (DOEA) – A Florida government agency that provides a wide variety of services to elderly Florida residents. The CARES unit, which is part of the DOEA, is involved in determining the medical needs of all Medicaid applicants in either skilled nursing facilities or assisted living facilities.

geriatric care manager (GCM) – An individual who assists the elderly and the elder's family in providing for the elder's care needs. Geriatric care managers often have backgrounds in social work and nursing.

gift – A transfer of property in which no consideration is given in return for the property. If there is consideration received, but the consideration is less than fair market value, the transfer of the property would then be considered a part sale, part gift.

Gift Tax Return (IRS Form 709) – The IRS form on which a person reports gifts they have given in amounts over $13,000 to any one person in any calendar year.

guardianship – The court-ordered process of the administration of the affairs of an incapacitated individual. Guardianship is typically an expensive and time consuming process and can be avoided with a properly executed durable power of attorney.

health care surrogate – A legal document in which an individual appoints someone else to authorize medical treatment and make medical decisions for them.

hospice – An organization that assists individuals and their family members deal with severe illnesses and end-of-life issues. Hospice provides services to individuals in hospitals, individuals living in the community, as well as individuals living in residential facilities, such as nursing homes.

income allocation (diversion) – The amount of income that can be diverted to the community spouse each month from the Medicaid recipient's income. The amount of income allocated to the community spouse can be increased, based on the total shelter expenses of the community spouse.

income cap – The monthly gross income limit in states that have an income cap for Medicaid.

institutionalized spouse (IS) – The spouse who is a resident of a skilled nursing facility or an assisted living facility.

Lady Bird deed (*See* enhanced life estate deed.)

level of care — The medical needs-based requirements for Medicaid. A Medicaid applicant's level of care is verified by the Florida Department of Elder Affairs CARES team, which determines appropriate placement for the Medicaid applicant in a skilled nursing facility or an assisted living facility.

life estate deed — A deed that allows a real estate owner to retain a life interest in real estate and transfer a remainder interest in the real estate to one or more beneficiaries. It is used to avoid probate. The transfer of the remainder interest under the deed would be considered a gift under the Medicaid rules, which would cause a disqualification period for Medicaid benefits. To avoid this problem, a Lady Bird deed can be used.

living trust — A popular estate planning document that enables a person to pass an estate to the beneficiaries of the estate without probate. A living trust has similarities to a testamentary will, in that beneficiaries of the estate are named in the event of the person's death. Living trusts, however, have several advantages over wills, including probate avoidance, incapacity planning and privacy.

living will — A legal document that deals with end-of-life issues. A living will in Florida covers three types of conditions — A persistent vegetative state, an end-stage condition or a terminal condition. If the attending physician and one other physician make one of these diagnoses, the person with a living will has directed that no life-prolonging medical treatments be pursued.

maximum monthly maintenance income allowance — The maximum total income the community spouse can receive (absent an appeal to fair hearing) with the combined total of the community spouse's income, with the institutionalized spouse's income allocation. The 2012 maximum monthly maintenance needs allowance is $2,841

Medicaid Qualifying Annuity – A specially structured, single-premium, immediate annuity with no cash value. It is non-transferable, nonassignable, irrevocable, with a term of equal to or less than the annuitant's life expectancy under the Social Security life expectancy tables. The Deficit Reduction Act of 2005 requires that the state of Florida be named as the primary beneficiary of the annuity to repay Medicaid benefits paid out on behalf of the annuitant.

Medicaid spend-down – The process of spending down countable assets, by privately paying the nursing home or assisted living facility bill, to gradually arrive below the Medicaid asset limit. A primary goal of Medicaid planning is to avoid the Medicaid spend-down.

Minimum monthly maintenance income allowance – The minimum total dollar amount of income the community spouse will receive from both the community spouse's income sources and the institutionalized spouse's income. In 2012 the minimum monthly maintenance allowance is $1,839 per month.

Omnibus Budget Reconciliation Act of 1993 (OBRA '93) – A federal law signed by President Clinton in 1993. The law provides that, as a general rule, assets held in trusts will be considered countable assets for Medicaid purposes. It contains two exceptions to that general rule: trusts for disabled individuals under 65 and pooled trusts for disabled individuals. OBRA '93 is also the legislation that authorizes Qualified Income Trusts.

patient responsibility – The portion of the Medicaid recipient's monthly income that must be paid to the facility. Typical deductions from patient responsibility include: the personal needs allowance ($35 per month for the Institutional Care Program and $54 per month for the Medicaid Waiver program), a deduction for the cost of secondary health insurance, and a deduction for any income allocated for the support of the community spouse.

penalty divisor (*See* divestment penalty division.)

personal needs allowance – The amount of income that a nursing home or assisted living facility resident can withhold from their payment of patient responsibility to the facility each month. The personal needs allowance for the institutionalized care program (ICP) is $35 per month; the personal needs allowance for the Medicaid Waiver Program is $54 per month.

personal services contract – A legal contract that can be executed by the Medicaid applicant to pay one or more individuals who are involved in the care of the individual. The personal services contract must be reasonable, and it must be based on the person's age, life expectancy, and the qualifications of the care givers to provide care. A personal services contract is an effective way to shelter assets to obtain Medicaid benefits.

power of attorney – A document that gives a person legal authority to act on another person's behalf. When a person creates such a document, they are called the principal, and the person to whom the principal gives this authority is called the attorney-in-fact. If the principal creates a durable power of attorney, the document will continue in effect even if the principal becomes incapacitated.

probate – A time-consuming and expensive court-ordered process that occurs when an individual dies with a will. (If a person dies without a will, the process is called an administration.) When people die owning assets in just their name, probate proceedings must be established to transfer title out of the deceased individual's name and into the name of the beneficiaries. Medicaid can recover against any nonexempt assets that go through either probate or an administration.

Qualified Income Trust (formerly called a Miller Trust) – Authorized under the Omnibus Budget and Reconciliation Act of 1993 (OBRA '93), a Qualified Income Trust is required to be established and funded monthly if the Medicaid applicant's gross monthly income exceeds the income cap in Florida.

Qualified Medicare Beneficiary (QMB) – A special state program that provides assistance to certain individuals with low income and limited assets. A person eligible as a QMB must be eligible to receive Medicare Part A, as well as meeting other requirements, similar to the basic three part test for Medicaid. Once eligible as a QMB, the recipient is entitled to financial assistance to pay for Medicare premiums as well as other deductibles.

Railroad Retirement Pension – A pension for individuals who have worked for a railroad for a certain period of time. It may also be available for some of the railroad worker's family members. As with the Social Security system, railroad retirees are eligible for Medicare benefits, and Railroad Retiree Benefits can be paid to railroad workers who have become disabled.

Request for Assistance (RFA) – The formal name for a Medicaid application. The filing of a Request for Assistance with the Florida Department of Children and Families (or the Florida Department of Elder Affairs) is the formal start of the Medicaid application process.

retroactive Medicaid benefits – Medicaid benefits may be retroactive for potentially up to 90 days prior to the date of the Medicaid application (for both the Institutional Care Program and for the Medicaid Waiver program). To receive retroactive Medicaid benefits, all Medicaid requirements must be fulfilled and verified for each prior month.

share of cost – A certain percentage of a Medicaid recipient's income that some Medicaid programs require to be spent, each month on medical care, before the Medicaid recipient is entitled to receive Medicaid benefits during any given month.

shelter expenses – The community spouse's housing expenses, such as rent, mortgage payments, lot rent, condominium maintenance fees, property taxes, property insurance, and water, sewage and electric bills. If the community spouse's shelter expenses exceed the shelter standard, the community spouse will be entitled to an increase in monthly income allocation from the institutionalized spouse.

shelter standard – The dollar figure that the community spouse's shelter expenses must exceed for the community spouse to receive an increase in income allocation over the minimum maintenance needs allowance.

SHINE – An acronym for an organization called "Serving Health Insurance Needs of Elders." SHINE is a volunteer organization that is part of the Florida Department of Elder Affairs. SHINE volunteers provide free counseling to elders and their family members for questions they have regarding health insurance, prescription drug programs, long-term care insurance, Medicare and Medicaid.

skilled nursing facility (SNF) – A state-licensed, residential facility that provides 24-hour nursing care for elderly, disabled, inured or sick individuals.

Social Security Disability Income (SSDI) – A Social Security benefit program for individuals, under the age of 65, who have previously worked and paid into the Social Security system for a certain minimum period of time. A person meeting these previous requirements will become eligible for SSDI when they become physically or mentally disabled. To be classified as disabled, the individuals must establish that they are unable to work as a result of the disability for a minimum of 12 months, or they must establish that the disability is expected to end only as the result of death. As a general rule, a person who is receiving SSDI benefits will also automatically meet the level of care requirement for Medicaid.

Special Needs Trust – A trust for disabled individuals under the age of 65. This type of trust is authorized under OBRA '93.

Special Needs Pooled Trust – Authorized under the Omnibus Budget and Reconciliation Act of 1993, a trust used to shelter a Medicaid applicant's assets so they can obtain Medicaid and other public benefits. Upon the death of the Medicaid beneficiary, any funds left in the trust must either be used to repay the Medicaid benefits paid out to the individual, or the funds must remain in the trust.

spousal refusal (assignment of rights to support) – A strategy, authorized by Florida law, that allows one spouse of a married couple to obtain Medicaid benefits, even if both spouses greatly exceed the allowable asset limits for Medicaid. If a spousal refusal strategy is used, the state of Florida reserves the right to recover Medicaid benefits paid out.

Supplemental Security Income (SSI) – Social Security payments made to disabled, blind or over-65 individuals with limited assets and income sources. As a general rule, a person who is receiving SSI benefits will also automatically meet the level of care requirement for Medicaid. With SSI, there is no requirement that the SSI beneficiary has ever paid into the Social Security system. However, if a person receiving SSI later receives too much income or too many assets from other sources, the recipient will lose eligibility for SSI benefits.

BIBLIOGRAPHY

Deficit Reduction Act of 2005

Florida Administrative Code

Florida Bar Association

Florida Economic Self-Sufficiency Public Assistance Policy Manual

Florida State Constitution

Florida Statutes

Floridabar.org

Internal Revenue Code

Omnibus Budget Reconciliation Act of 1993

Social Security Act

United States Code, Title 42

About the Author

John R. Frazier

John R. Frazier graduated Cum Laude from Hampden-Sydney College in Virginia with a B.A. in Economics in 1986. He received his Master's degree in Business Administration from Virginia Tech in 1994; graduated Cum Laude from the University of Toledo, College of Law in 1997; and received his LL.M. in Taxation from the University of Florida, College of Law in 1998.

He is licensed to practice Law in both Florida and Georgia, and he practices primarily in the fields of Elder Law, Medicaid Planning, Veterans Benefits Law, Estate Planning, Asset Protection, Taxation, and Business Organizations.

John is admitted to practice before the United States Court of Appeals for Veterans Claims, and he is accredited by the Veterans Administration to assist VA claimants present, prepare and prosecute claims with the VA. He is also a member of the National Organization of Veterans Advocates, Inc., the National Academy of Elder Law Attorneys, the Academy of Florida Elder Law Attorneys, and the Florida Bar Elder Law Section.

As the son of a physician and military officer, and with four brothers, John traveled widely in the U.S.A. and abroad while growing up. John's exposure to different cultures has created a lifelong interest in learning about other regions of the world. His current interests include exercising, hiking in the Blue Ridge Mountains of Virginia, the study of Latin America, Spanish music and reading.

John R. Frazier can be reached through his website:

www.EstateLegalPlanning.com